Badiou
and the
Philosophers

Badiou and the Philosophers

Interrogating 1960s
French Philosophy

EDITED AND TRANSLATED

BY TZUCHIEN THO AND

GIUSEPPE BIANCO

BLOOMSBURY
LONDON • NEW DELHI • NEW YORK • SYDNEY

Bloomsbury Academic

An imprint of Bloomsbury Publishing Plc

50 Bedford Square	175 Fifth Avenue
London	New York
WC1B 3DP	NY 10010
UK	USA

www.bloomsbury.com

First published 2013

British Library Cataloguing-in-Publication Data
A catalogue record for this book is available from the British Library.

ISBN: HB: 978–1–4411–8485–6
PB: 978–1–4411–9521–0
ePub: 978–1–4411–0959–0
ePDF: 978–1–4411–9988–1

Library of Congress Cataloging-in-Publication Data
Badiou, Alain.
Badiou and the philosophers : interrogating 1960s French philosophy / edited and translated by Tzuchien Tho and Giuseppe Bianco.
p. cm.
Includes bibliographical references and index.
ISBN 978-1-4411-8485-6 (hardcover)– ISBN 978-1-4411-9521-0 (pbk.)– ISBN 978-1-4411-0959-0 (epub)– ISBN 978-1-4411-9988-1 (ebook pdf) 1. Philosophy, French–20th century. 2. Philosophers–France–Interviews. 3. Badiou, Alain–Interviews. 4. Badiou, Alain. I. Tho, Tzuchien. II. Bianco, Giuseppe. III. Title.
B2421.B2713 2013
194–dc23
2012030172

Typeset by Fakenham Prepress Solutions, Fakenham, Norfolk NR21 8NN
Printed and bound in India

CONTENTS

Acknowledgments vii
Editors' and translator's introduction ix

1 Philosophy and its history (with Jean Hyppolite) 1

2 Philosophy and science (with Georges Canguilhem) 15

3 Philosophy and sociology (with Raymond Aron) 33

4 Philosophy and psychology (with Michel Foucault) 47

5 Philosophy and language (with Paul Ricœur) 61

6 Philosophy and truth (with Georges Canguilhem, Dina Dreyfus, Michel Foucault, Jean Hyppolite, and Paul Ricœur) 79

7 Philosophy and ethics (with Michel Henry) 99

8 Model and structure (with Michel Serres) 111

9 Teaching philosophy through television
   (with excerpts from Jean Hyppolite, Georges
   Canguilhem, Raymond Aron, Michel Foucault,
   and Paul Ricœur. Alain Badiou by telephone and
   Dina Dreyfus in the studio) 139

Appendices:

A Short biographies of participants 153

B The critical value of images
   Alain Badiou (1993) 159

Index 161

ACKNOWLEDGMENTS

"Philosophy and its History", "Philosophy and Science", "Philosophy and Sociology", "Philosophy and Psychology", "Philosophy and Language", "Philosophy and Truth", "Teaching Philosophy through Television" and "The Critical Value of Images" were translated from the French transcripts of those interviews that is available in print in a special volume of the journal *Cahiers Philosophiques*, 55 (June 1993). A subset of these texts had appeared as teaching materials produced by *Dossiers pédagogiques de la Radio-Télévision scolaire* in 1965. A modified version of "Philosophie et psychologie" was published in Foucault's collected works *Dits et Écrits*, Vol. I (Paris: Seuil, 1966), 546–67. Transcription and Translation of "Philosophy and Ethics" and "Model and Structure" from videos made available by the *Centre National de Documentation Pédagogique*.

Since "Model and Structure" contain extensive use of Molière's *Don Juan*, we also need to acknowledge our use of Graverley and Maclean's translation published by Oxford University Press. MOLIERE: DON JUAN & OTHER PLAYS translated by Graveley & Maclean (2008) pp. 33, 63–4, 72–5, 91. By permission of Oxford University Press.

We are thankful to Bernard Canguilhem (Canguilhem estate), Claude Chippaux-Hyppolite and Alain Chippaux (Hyppolite estates), Dominique Schnapper (Aron estate), Gregori Jean and Jean Leclercq of the Fonds Ricœur, Catherine Goldenstein of the Fonds Michel Henry and Gallimard publishers (Foucault estate) for their permission to translate and publish these texts. We are also grateful to the *Centre National de Documentation Pédagogique* for their permission to use these materials. Much thanks also go to Alain Badiou for his permission and encouragement for undertaking this project.

EDITORS' AND TRANSLATOR'S INTRODUCTION

Sailin' on: Voyages in French philosophy 1957–67

"According to this interrogation, thought is forced to weigh anchor and to set sail on an uncertain sea; thought is for itself that quasi-other that everyone is, in Borreil's view, for everyone else. The nomadic image is inscribed from the outset in that singular style, which never asserts anything except under the rule of an interrogation, and interposes between the interrogation and the response the interval between the morning departure and the evening halt."[1]

Socratic interlocutor

In the epigraph above, Alain Badiou speaks of Jean Borreil, his colleague at the University of Paris VIII, and remarks on his admiration for his style of interrogations. These are not questions aimed at interpretation, as Badiou insists, but direct interrogations that mark the interlocutor and implicate her within a nomadic movement of thought. Badiou's elegy to his friend and colleague first pronounced at the *College Internationale de Philosophie* was collected in a series of essays on French philosophical figures in 2008 as *Petit Panthéon Portatif*, a *Pocket Pantheon*. In this volume, Alain Badiou pointed his readers to a range of figures who have served as mentors, teachers, role models, friends, and adversaries. Some of these figures are household names like Jean-Paul Sartre, others are intellectual supernovas like Jacques Derrida and also a number of other names that might have otherwise faded into the dust of the archives like Jean Borreil and Gilles Châtelet.

On this occasion Badiou highlights a precise year, 1965. He remarks on the exceptional set of thinkers who served as professors for the generation who, in 1965, were in their 20s and 30s. The mid-1960s would then serve as a turning point not only for French philosophy in general but also for Badiou himself. This is the turning point that would be marked by the movement, cemented after 1968, toward what François Cusset has highlighted and analyzed in his book as "French Theory".[2] We might here provide caution that this mid-60s period was not yet "French Theory" but rather still "French Philosophy" with the trappings of its pre-1968 academicism and classicism. Part of this transformation was the call for Badiou's participation in the televised series represented in this volume. This classicism was not yet contaminated by the instrumental use, made by the "nouveaux philosophes"[3] starting from the late 1970s, of the "thinker's" body and presence in the social space through the use of the television media.

In 1964, after having consulted Georges Canguilhem and Jean Hyppolite, Dina Dreyfus asked Alain Badiou to play the role of the "socratic interlocutor"[4] in the television series "Le temps des philosophes." At this moment, Badiou, a secondary school teacher in Reims, had just published his first novel, *Almagestes*, whose first chapter, dedicated to his spouse, had appeared in the January issue of Sartre's journal, *Les Temps modernes*, preceded by a short introduction written by Simone de Beauvoir.[5] While presenting the book on the television show "Lecture pour tous,"[6] Badiou announced that he was already writing the second volume of a trilogy called *Trajectoire Inverse, Portulans*. Given the excellent reception from the press, and even encouragement from Sartre himself,[7] many of Badiou's peers, like the 'sevriénne'[8] Cathérine Clément, were sure that he would have become "the big novelist that everyone was waiting for, a new Julien Gracq."[9] It was in the model of the Sartre of *Nausea* that Badiou wanted to be a novelist, "a natural French model, inherited from Voltaire and Rousseau, a model in which philosophy and literature were undistinguished."[10] This didn't happen.

In the autumn of 1965 François Regnault, four years younger than Badiou, arrives in Reims to teach at the same school after having spent four years at the *Ecole Normale* and one year in military service. Regnault arrives with news about the seminars of Jacques Lacan and Louis Althusser at the *Ecole* and informs Badiou, who had been estranged from the Parisian and *Normalien* scene since 1961, of the project that will become, a few months later, *Les Cahiers pour l'Analyse*. Separated from the *Ecole Normale* at this moment, Badiou would eventually be drawn into the currents of this nomadism of French philosophy through a series of political engagements, the imperative of anti-theoreticism and the antagonisms of deconstruction.

Called back to the capital through this project, a series of other engagements, friendships, and collaboration began to overtake Badiou's considered career as a school teacher and novelist. These were the encounters that would eventually push him into the currents of what was already stirring in 1964 under the paving stones of the *Quartier Latin*.

French philosophy

As editors and translators, the temptation in introducing this collection of interviews is one of getting carried away, as it were, by the enticing currents of retrospective over-determination. That is, the temptation of making sheer correlations causal, rendering the contingent necessary and treating associations as influence. As editors before a book project, we were no doubt setting out in full sail: a full set of the most notable French philosophers of the post-war period. Some of these figures were already highly influential at the time of these interviews and some will soon become strong voices. We find here also the central and dynamic participation of a 27-year-old Alain Badiou, lanky, serious, and quick to turn a phrase. The conception and supervision of the project by Dina Dreyfus also give a snapshot of the rare "behind-the-scenes" story of the constellations of French philosophy between the philosophical world of the French universities, a general public nourished in the philosophical culture of its St Germain celebrity writers and poets, and the many links with pedagogical institutions through the role that philosophers assigned to themselves in producing the modern citizen-subjects of the early fifth Republic.

Of course this volume is just as much a snapshot of those professors who marked their influence during the early 1960s as that of Badiou himself, who undertook a maturity in the decades following. As we now know Badiou was both a resistant figure of the post-'68 tendency of the transition of French philosophy into *theory* as well as an implicated party. It is then not only as an allegory but also as narration that Badiou's biography will allow us to understand his trajectory since the 1960s as a surface on which these very shaky transformations in French philosophy might be interpreted. As such, we find in Badiou an anchor for which these sailings in French philosophy can be read, one that is based not in transformation but in the conservative notion of preserving tradition, tied to pedagogy, tied to national curriculum, and finally tied to the *Ecole Normale Supérieure* as philosophical institution.

In an Anglophone context, the impression of French philosophy is not one that could be displaced with such a simple volume; there is no doubt that the content of these interviews collected here will be partially understood as a pre-history of what will become the dominant themes and problematics in the immediately post-1968 generation. In resisting this post-1968 determination, however, we attempt to provide another picture, one traced through the figure of Badiou, born at the eve of the Second World War and whose entire upbringing and education will be determined by the material conditions, social effects, and intellectual events of this wartime and immediately post-war context. As a biography where these events were inscribed, Badiou might be read not only as the young interlocutor of Canguilhem, Hyppolite, Foucault, and these other established figures in 1965, but also the allegorical representative of a whole generation that would eventually face the political and philosophical choices placed before them in 1968. This biography is thus an important aperture, one of many to be sure, for viewing the context of this transition from French "philosophy" to French "theory." Yet, in resisting the attempt to look "backwards" from the late 1960s and 1970s, we have tried to provide in the following a series of perspectives that might allow us to look "forward."

Sartre: An apprenticeship in philosophy

Badiou was born 17 January 1937 in Rabat where, since 1929, his father Raymond had been teaching mathemathics in one of the city's secondary schools. Raymond Badiou had studied at the *Ecole Normale* and belonged to the same cohort (1924) as Sartre, Canguilhem, and Nizan, not to mention some of the mathematicians who will later form the allonymic mathematical society Nicolas Bourbaki.[11] Since 1934 the elder Badiou had been a member of the *Section Française de l'Internationale Ouvrière* (SFIO) and from 1935 to 1936 took part in Rabat's antifascist group '*Etudes et Actions*'. After the French defeat, the family moved to Toulouse in 1941, where Raymond started teaching in a secondary school and entered into the Résistance as a member of the clandestine SFIO. When *Libération* finally arrived, Raymond Badiou became mayor of Toulouse, where he instituted a series of strongly socialist policies, distinguishing himself as the left wing of the party opposed to Léon Blum and favoring a rapprochement between the SFIO and the *Parti Communiste Française* (PCF). Raymond participated, with Sartre, in the project, the *Rassemblement Démocratique Révolutionnaire* (1948–9) of an alternative radical left that would oppose both the Stalinism of the PCF and reformism of the SFIO. From 1956, following the line of Pierre Mendes-France, he also opposed the Algerian war and opposed the eventual support given by his party to De Gaulle.[12]

In 1955, a 17–year-old Badiou, initially oriented towards a career either as a forest ranger or as an actor, read *The Imaginary*, *The Emotions*, and finally *Being and Nothingness*[13] of Sartre. This turned him toward philosophy.[14] This initiation to philosophy through Sartre was common to many of his elder colleagues: Gérard Grenel, Claude Lanzman, Michel Tournier, Gilles Deleuze. During the summer of the same year, after having read Simone de Beauvoir's review of Merleau-Ponty's *The Adventure of the Dialectics*[15], in which she defended Sartre from the criticisms of Merleau-Ponty, Badiou wrote her a letter in which he agreed with her position. Badiou made his way to Paris from the south at the end of 1956 to prepare for the entrance exam for the *Ecole Normale* at the *Henri IV* secondary school. Here, Badiou met De Beauvoir several times to discuss about philosophy and politics and became "an absolutely convinced Sartrean."[16] Badiou's first novel, *Almagestes*, includes a series of dialogues between four characters (Bérard, Fréville, Dastaing, and Chantal)[17] probably inspired by this period at the *Ecole Normale*. Especially in theme[18] and in form, the notion of the "exterior monologue"[19] in this novel was coated in Sartrean language.

Badiou had been struck by the idea of the Sartrean formula: "Consciousness is a being such that in its being, its being is in question insofar as this being implies a being other than itself,"[20] contained in *Being and Nothingness*, and he will remain faithful to this formula that asserts an intentional consciousness without interiority. This notion of consciousness implied that "psychology is the enemy of thought"[21] and whose being was in turn one of projection, pretension and injunction. Like many others of his generation Badiou found in Sartre, in the latter's "existential humanism," the idea that "the human being does not exist except insofar as it overcomes its humanity."[22]

This admiration for Sartre will be constant throughout Badiou's whole intellectual itinerary.[23] This was the case even after 1966 when he began working in close relation with Althusser, who had shown his hostility against existentialism since 1948.[24] In the late 70s, Badiou would remark that one stills prefers Sartre the idealist on the streets against the state over Althusser the PCF party intellectual.[25]

As such, Badiou will later say that one could not become philosopher without having been the disciple of someone.[26] This absolute master was for Badiou none other than Sartre. Speaking of the period, Badiou would remark that it was in the model provided by Sartre that he could entertain this heterogenity of topics, a "polygraphy", from film, mathematics, music, and politics.[27]

The Algerian war

During this period Badiou published a series of short texts in a student journal, *Vin Nouveau*, which was animated by the left-wing Catholics of the *Ecole Normale*.[28] The journal, which was conceived as the continuation of the *Cahiers Talas*, was slowly distancing itself from the chaplain of the *Ecole* and received some of the most brilliant students, most of whom were not Catholic, at the *Ecole*. Here Badiou published on literature,[29] opera,[30] film,[31] poetry,[32] and, finally, politics.[33]

Badiou, who had never been part of the '*talas*',[34] was clearly not attracted by the religious orientation of *Vin Nouveau*, but rather by the journal's political engagement against the war in Algeria. At the end of 1956, a few months after Badiou's arrival in Paris, *Vin Nouveau* published an issue on Algeria,[35] entitled "Urgence pour l'Algérie," where the collaborators analyzed the critical situation of the indigenous inhabitants of the French colony and called for a peaceful resolution to the conflict. Since his arrival in Paris, Badiou was engaged in a series of demonstrations on the Boulevard Saint-Michel which faced severe police violence.[36] During 1956–7, with Emmanuel Terray,[37] his schoolmate at the *Ecole*, he joined the SFIO and become secretary of the sub-section of the Rue d'Ulm. Like his father, young Alain participated in the minority of the party against the Algerian war. In 1958 both Badiou and Terray left the SFIO because of its mainstream position in support of the Algerian war. They first joined the Parti Socialiste Autonome (PSA) then the Parti Socialiste Unifié (PSU). During early 1961, Badiou was sent on a journalistic assignment to Belgium, accompanied by his good friend and fellow Sartrean Pierre Verstraeten, to report on a massive strike.[38]

Badiou's political engagement during the 1950s could not but reinforce his admiration for Jean-Paul Sartre and was even *motivated* by Sartre.[39] The "political" Sartre of the mid-1950s was in fact very different from the deeply "metaphysical" or "literary" one of the 40s that Deleuze, Lanzmann, Tournier, and Grenel admired during those years. Sartre's journal, *Les Temps modernes*, which occupied the central stage of French intellectual field,[40] was, since 1953, engaged in the struggle against colonialism in Indochina[41]. Since the end of the 1940s, Sartre expressed positions favourable to the independence of Tunisia and Morocco. In May 1955, *Les Temps modernes* published an article by Jean Cohen and Mohamed Chérif Sahli entitled "L'Algérie n'est pas la France"[42] and later, in December 1955, Francis Jeanson, a close associate of the journal, published the book *L'Algérie hors la loi*. Finally in March 1956 Sartre published in *Les Temps modernes* the text of a powerful talk that he gave two months before entitled "Colonialism is a system."[43] In 1956 Sartre broke with both the

SFIO, because of Guy Mollet's engagement in the intensification of the war, and the PCF which, during the same year, approved the Soviet invasion of Hungary. From 1956 to 1962, in his interventions against the Algerian war, Sartre seems to have discovered the importance of a new political subject in the figure of the colonized that would take us beyond that of the proletariat. Until the end of the Algerian war, Sartre would continue to denounce colonialism as a system, condemn the use of torture,[44] and underline the hypocrisy of the French, its press, and its political discourse.

Badiou, born in Morocco, could not but follow suit. Many of his cohorts at the *Ecole* took action against the war. This generation of students who began higher education in the 1950s were very different from the generation that preceded them. Michel Foucault (1947), Gérard Grenel (1949), Jacques Derrida (1951), and Pierre Bourdieu (1951) all agree that while they were studying or finishing their studies at the *Ecole Normale*, at the beginning of the 50s, Sartre was considered old-fashioned and few paid much attention to the latter's works. In his autobiography, Althusser writes that, starting from 1945, at the *Ecole Normale*, "It was fashionable to pretend to despise Sartre ..."[45] Even students at the Sorbonne of this earlier generation like Gilles Deleuze, Michel Tournier, Oliver Revault d'Allonnes, and Gilles Châtelet quickly abandoned Sartre's phenomenology at the end of the 40s either because of the sentiment that the model of the engaged intellectual was ineffectual, or because their ties to the PCF did not allow them to side with existentialism which was considered to be bourgeois ideology. As Edward Baring has recently shown in his book on Derrida,[46] the Sartrean passion that very often motivated the "conversion" to philosophy of different generations quickly evaporated around 1953 and everyone took up either a more "scientific" version of phenomenology, Heideggerism, or Marxism (or a combination thereof).[47]

The Algerian "events" would be a flashpoint that would change the climate of the intellectual field and revive an interest in Sartre as a model. This profoundly affected Badiou insofar as it was through the project of anti-colonialization that a rigid imperial systematicity is pitted against the emergence of the subject's practical freedom. It was thus through anti-imperialism and the activities against the Algerian war that this Sartrean dialectic of system and singularity would inform Badiou's maturation.[48]

Decolonization, anthropology, formalization

At the end of 1955 while Badiou was studying for the *Ecole Normale* entrance exam, Claude Lévi-Strauss published his *Tristes Tropiques* that, some months before, had been anticipated by a fragment that was published in *Les Temps modernes*.[49] The book constituted something of an intellectual event partly due to the author's refusal of the "Plume d'Or" literary prize in November 1956.[50]

Lévi-Strauss' impact was a significant one and could be deeply felt in this young generation of students that were getting back in touch with the "political" Sartre so profoundly engaged in anti-colonization and the rejection of Stalinism. In 1957 Badiou and two of his close friends, Emmanuel Terray and Pierre Verstraeten, read Lévi-Strauss' *The Elementary Structures of Kindship* with close attention.[51] The effects of this book on each one of them will be different. Terray would slowly abandon philosophy for anthropology and left France for Africa. He would eventually write *Le marxisme devant les societies primitives* in 1969.[52] Verstraeten attempted a mediation between Sartre and Lévi-Strauss.[53] Badiou was in turn probably more interested by the formal concepts used by Lévi-Strauss and especially in the theory of groups used in *The Elementary Structures of Kinship*.[54] This interesting mathematical dimension of the book was itself the result of André Weil's friendship with Lévi-Strauss while both were in exile in the United States during the war. Weil returned to France after the war to develop the mathematical group Nicolas Bourbaki and become one of the most influential mathematicians in the late 20th century. It was perhaps on the basis of this interest for Lévi-Strauss that Badiou saw the open intersections between mathematics and structuralism. It was however through his spouse Françoise[55] that he was eventually introduced to a group of mathematicians, among whom was Maurice Matieu,[56] someone with whom he would develop a long friendship.

Besides these personal trajectories between the end of the 1950s and the beginning of the 1960s we witness a series of publications concerning formal sciences in relation to phenomenology. Until the early 1950s the interest of phenomenology focused on the late Husserl, the analysis of intersubjectivity, and the prereflexive experience of the world to the "existential" interpretations of phenomenology of Sartre, Merleau-Ponty, and Ricœur. Albert Lautman and Jean Cavaillès, who both worked on the epistemology of mathematics from a phenomenological perspective, both perished during the war. During the second half of the 1950s the situation went through a slow change: in 1957 Suzanne Bachelard, daughter of the famous epistemologist, published her Ph.D. dissertation on Husserl's logic and, the following year, a book on phenomenology of mathematics[57]. In 1960, a pupil of Jean Cavaillès teaching in Rennes, Gilles-Gaston Granger, published an important book on human sciences and formalism[58]. In 1962, Jules Vuillemin, also a student of Cavaillès and teaching in Clermont-Ferrand, published *Philosophie de l'algebre*[59] which was anticipated, in 1959, by an important article on phenomenology and formalism, "Le problème phénoménologique: intentionalité et réflexion."[60] In 1962 Derrida published his translation of Husserl's *Origin of Geometry*[61] and Roger Martin, librarian of the *Ecole Normale* from 1950 until 1964, published his edition of a collection of a series of Cavaillès' essays, *Philosophie mathématique.*[62] Two years later Martin will publish, in Hyppolite's collection "Epimethée," his *Logique contemporaine et formalisation*. Michel Serres was at that moment working on his dissertation on Leibniz and mathematics while writing on formalization in modern philosophy. All these figures were either teaching at the Sorbonne or giving lectures at the *Ecole Normale* under the invitation of Hyppolite and Althusser.

During the last three years of his studies at the *Ecole Normale*, Badiou then witnessed an ongoing reflection on the foundation of mathematics. These figures approached foundational questions through a philosophy informed by phenomenology. However many of the new generation of thinkers like Gilles-Gaston Granger, Jules Vuillemin, and Roger Martin were skeptical of this approach, much like their mentor Cavaillès. Cavaillès had established the position, in his posthumously published *La Logique et théorie de la science*, that the developements of mathematics cannot be grounded on the transcendental sphere of a phenomenological consciousness.

In 1960 Badiou passed the *agrégation* and wrote his DES [diplôme d'études supérieures] thesis, supervised by Georges Canguilhem, on the *Structures démonstratives dans les deux premiers livres de l'Ethique de Spinoza*[63]. At this time the idea of creating a "Spinoza Group"[64] had not yet occurred to Althusser; Badiou's choice of this topic was probably tied to the *agrégation* programme, to Gueroult's lectures at the *Collège de France*,[65] but also to the Spinozist orientation of Jean Cavaillès' later work, *Sur la logique et la théorie de la science*,[66] posthumously published and edited by Canguilhem in 1947.[67] The same year Gilles-Gaston Granger would publish "Jean Cavaillès ou la montée vers Spinoza," a review of his mentor's book that alluded to one of Lautman's titles, which would include the remark that *Sur la logique et la théorie de la science* was a fragment of what would have become Cavaillès' *Ethics*. One could say something similar about Badiou's DES thesis, a fragment that, at least according to Terray[68], would have been a draft to the 10th meditation of *Being and Event*.

From mathème to poème

This move toward a concern for the foundation of science and on formalization in the philosophical field was curiously accompanied by something that, at first glance, might have seemed to have an echo in these same tendencies in the literary field. It was in reality something completely independent from it.

At the beginning of the 1950s, the intellectual French field was dominated by Sartre and *Les Temps modernes*, by the idea of the novelist as an engaged individual, free and responsible for his creations and their effects on society. In the middle of the 50s however there was a transformation of both the model of the engaged writer and the question of literary forms that were established in the 1940s. This change began stirring within the same journals that promoted existentialism, like the *Les Temps modernes*, *Critique*, and the publisher Gallimard. Writers started moving over to publishers like Minuit and Seuil. In 1953 Roland Barthes published his *Writing Degree Zero*, a collection of essays with an implicit opposition to Sartre, to the "well-behaved writing of revolutionaries," and which praised the work of writers who "created a colorless writing, freed from all bondage to a pre-ordained state of language."[69]

The same year an agronomist, Alain Robbe-Grillet, published his first novel, *The Erasers* [*Les Gommes*], that Barthes, in an article for *Critique* of the following year, welcomed as the example of a new experimental writing, opposed to the petty bourgeois novel, an objective and "superficial" writing freed from psychology and from both the dimensions of depth and breadth. Barthes will later gather a series of contributions published in journals such as *Les lettres françaises* and *Esprit* in a volume, *Mythologies*[70], in which he applied structuralism to the analysis of quotidian life as a system of signs that, in turn, composes a system of beliefs, a *doxa*.

In the same year of the publication of *Mythologies*, 1957, Nathalie Sarraute republished her novel *Tropisms*. In the previous year she had published a collection of essays on literature, *The Age of Suspicion*, where she stated her refusal of the conventions of the traditional novel. Here she promoted a form of writing that would suppress any differentiation between dialogue and description in order to grant the reader a crucial role in the interpretation of the text. This in turn stressed the significance of words themselves. It is also in 1957 that Michel Butor, trained as a philosopher, published his third novel, *The Modification*, in which he followed in this same movement of the deconstruction and critique of the traditional forms of the novel.

In the same year Emile Heriot, in a famous article published 22 November 1957 in *Le Monde*, spoke out against what he called, in contempt, the "*nouveau roman*" [new novel]. Around this time, Alain Robbe-Grillet published a series of essays on the novel, which will later be gathered in the 1963 collection *For a New Novel*. Robbe-Grillet rejected many of the established features of the novel such as plot, action, narrative, ideas, character, and psychological portraiture. He promoted a writing focused on a description of objects purified from any human predicate, radicalizing Barthes' "zero level" of writing. In 1955 Robbe-Grillet became the literary editor of Minuit publishers and helped cement the definition of writers of this "new novel."[71]

A bit later, around the beginning of the 1960s, a group of writers, including Raymond Queneau, Italo Calvino, and Georges Perec, created *OuLiPo* (*L'Ouvroir de littérature potentielle*) [workshop for potential literature], a group of writers who aimed at literary experiments using mathematical models and focusing on the description of things and events rather than on characters.

Finally in 1960 Philippe Sollers created the *Tel Quel* journal put out by the publisher Seuil. In the same vein as the "*nouveau roman*" the journal also contributed to an anti-Sartrean front in literature. It was oriented towards what Sollers called an "immanent praxis of text" and was opposed to the "extra-literary justification of literature."[72] Even though these new movements and discussions were concentrated around the novel, *Tel Quel* promoted poetry in a broader sense, including esoteric formalist writing (emphasis on syntax and sonority, puns, typography, and spatial arrangement) inspired by surrealism, Joyce and Mallarmé. The journal slowly moved away from the "*nouveau roman*" and manifested an interest in structuralism, in the human sciences, and in philosophy, first publishing an enthusiast review of Lévi-Strauss' *The Savage Mind* in 1962 and, a bit later, texts by Derrida, Foucault, Barthes, and the young novelist and philosopher Jean-Pierre Faye. It was in this movement that Sollers in 1963 inaugurated a *Tel Quel* book series at Seuil. It was thus not by chance that this same publishing house put out *Almagestes*, a text that attempted to bring together all the elements promoted by the group.

As Badiou pointed out later, this period dominated by "Robbe-Grillet, the *nouveau roman* and the *nouvelle vague* in cinema" provoked "the feeling of a kind of fundamental transformation of the entirety of intellectual givens" [*l'ensemble des données de l'intellectualité*].[73]

A short walk from Rue d'Ulm down Rue St Jacques

While events and discourses formed the general context of this period, the concrete influence of this earlier generation of thinkers was constituted by the 15–minute walk from the *Ecole Normale* to the Sorbonne and, eventually, to the *Collège de France*. Jean Hyppolite had served since 1954 as the director of the *Ecole Normale* and its regent.[74] After his translation of Hegel's *Phenomenology of the Spirit*, the publication of his commentary *Genesis and Structure of Hegel's Phenomenology of the Spirit*, and a few essays on Hegel and Marx at the beginning of the 1950s, Hyppolite, like many of his colleagues, was struck by a "Heideggerian lightning"[75] which influenced both the anti-humanism and the attention paid to language present in his second book on Hegel, *Logic and Existence*, published in 1952. Hyppolite taught a weekly course and turned the *Salle des Actes* at the *Ecole* into a gathering of diverse students and external auditors.[76] As director of the *Ecole* Hyppolite also encouraged political engagement as well as contemporary artistic forms like the musical work of Pierre Boulez and the *"nouveau roman."*[77] As Badiou would later recount, Hyppolite and Canguilhem were the *"protecteurs de la nouveauté"* [protectors of the novelty][78] and it was through their active guardianship that the major philosophical creations of the 1960s found a nest at the *Ecole*. In fact, since the 1950s Hyppolite, in collaboration with Althusser, following student interest, invited a series of lecturers to give talks in different domains of specialization: Canguilhem on philosophy and epistemology, Andé Ombredane on psychology, Jean Beaufret and Henri Birault on Heidegger, Jules Vuillemin and Michel Serres on modern philosophy, Victor Goldschmidt on ancient philosophy. At the same time, while students at the *Ecole* had generally not attended lectures at the Sorbonne, Althusser actively encouraged them take the short walk and participate in the courses of Paul Ricœur, Georges Canguilhem, and Raymond Aron.

Althusser had since 1949 been the *agrégé-répétiteur* (*caiman*) at the *Ecole* and had, from early 1950, been the general-secretary of the *Ecole*. His job description as *agrégé-répétiteur* was to give seminars in the preparation of the agrégation exam and to organize sporadic parallel seminars on topics in his own research.

It was in this function that in 1959, in addition to a series of lectures on political philosophy of the seventeenth and eighteenth centuries, Althusser also organized a seminar on psychoanalysis.[79] During the early 1950s, Althusser was also engaged in the *"Georges Politzer Cercle"*, named after the Marxist critic and reformer of psychology and psychoanalysis, which aimed, through a series of talks, at informing both communists and non-communists alike of "the possibilities of Marxist criticism."[80] It was in the former context of the seminar at the *Ecole* that Emmanuel Terray gave a seminar on "La psychanalyse des psychoses," probably inspired by Jean Laplanche's 1958 essay "A la recherche des principes d'une psychothérapie des psychoses."[81] It is also in this context that Badiou presented, in 1959, his first exposé on Lacan, based on the essays published in the latter's journal, *La Psychanalyse*.[82]

Although psychoanalysis was a center of focus for students of the *Ecole*, psychology was treated as a non-science. In 1947 Daniel Lagache, who had just been elected professor at the Sorbonne, created the first undergraduate degree program in psychology and published his famous *L'Unité de la psychologie*[83] two years later. At the same time, Ignace Meyerson attained full professorship at *Ecole pratique des hautes études en sciences sociales* in 1951 and created a center for research in "comparative psychology." A psychology of introspection had already been criticized by Sartre on the basis of phenomenology,[84] and a few years later had been treated by Heideggerians such as Beaufret and Birault as a sophisticated form of anthropologism.[85] At the end of 1956, it had been the object of the epistemological attacks from Georges Canguilhem in his famous talk "What is psychology?"[86] In the meantime, the party intellectuals of the PCF had condemned psychoanalysis as part of petty bourgeois ideology since the end of the 1940s. Psychology was, for a moment, through the works of Politzer, reintegrated in the Marxian apparatus but without great success. The result was that, as the psychologist Emile Jalley argued, the *Ecole Normale* was a milieu hostile to psychology since 1955. Alain Badiou, who entered the Ecole in 1956, considered, in mockery, that psychology was ridiculous and an obsolete leftover of knowledge.[87]

Althusser's activity during the years that Badiou passed at the *Ecole Normale* (1956–61) was very different from both the early 1950s and the 1960s. Althusser had often been absent because of his health and spoke very carefully due to his position in the PCF.[88] It is only in 1961 that Althusser began his cycle of intensive seminars with his students at *Ecole Normale*. He was promoted to associate professor in 1962 and organized seminars on the young Marx (1961–2), on the originis of structuralism (1962–3), on Lacan and psychoanalysis (1963–4) and on *The Capital* (1964–5). In 1964 Lacan was expelled from Sainte-Anne Hospital and it was Althusser who provided the psychoanalyst a new base, at the *Ecole*, for his teaching. In 1963, Pierre Bourdieu and Jean-Claude Passeron, two of Althusser's students, were invited by their teacher to start up their seminar on sociology at the *Ecole*. It is only at this moment that Althusser entered into a closer relation with Canguilhem and the latter's seminar at the Sorbonne.[89] This conjuncture will result in the intellectual effervescence at the *Ecole* which would eventually lead to the publication of *Reading Capital* and *For Marx* in 1965, to the creation of the *Cahiers marxistes-léninistes*, and of the *Cahiers pour l'analyse* in 1966.

In this exceptional period of Althusser's activity and the active environment that he fostered, Badiou had already left the *Ecole* and he was merely a "provincial general secretary of the PSU of the Marne region, a novelist." [90] He was far from the *Normalien* scene and, more in general, far from Paris, where the structuralist *querelle* had exploded. This explosion implied that both the Sartrean figure of the "total intellectual" and the "phenomenological" model of subjectivity were slowly disappearing from view. In the last chapter of Lévi-Strauss' *The Savage Mind* entitled "History and Dialectics" published in 1962, Lévi-Strauss harshly attacked the author of *Critique of Dialectical Reason* from several angles. He was opposed to Sartre's instrumentalization of his own work and criticized Sartre's privilege of history over other human sciences and, finally, on an epistemological level, he counterposed the structuralist paradigm of meaning to that of phenomenology. The task of the human sciences according to Lévi-Strauss was the one of "dissolving" the philosophical concept of "man" in order to explain phenomena. Lévi-Strauss' book had lain waste to any attempt at combining structuralism and the phenomenological model. Structuralism was not only an instrument to understand human phenomena but it implied a theory of knowledge and even an ontology that were incompatible with the phenomenological approach.

During the 1950s, philosophers such as Claude Lefort[91] and Jean Pouillon,[92] from *Les Temps modernes* editorial board, tried to combine structuralism with the Sartrean apparatus. Later, during 1962–3 two seminars on Lévi-Strauss' work took place, one organized by Althusser at the *Ecole Normale* and another organized by the editorial board of the *Esprit* journal around Paul Ricœur, who began to develop an interest in the status of language because of the latter's studies on hermeneutics[93]. Both seminars concluded that structuralism implied a Kantianism without subjectivity and was incompatible with phenomenology and humanist Marxism.

At around the same moment, two Lacanian psychoanalysts, Jean Laplanche and Serge Leclaire, presented their paper, "The Unconscious: A Psychoanalytic Study,"[94] at the Bonneval psychoanalysis conference, published in 1961 in *Les Temps modernes*. In the first part of this paper they criticized both Georges Politzer's and Sartre's idea of the unconscious, stating its incompatibility with the Lacanian idea of the unconscious structured like a language. This criticism provoked Althusser's evacuation of Politzer's contribution to Marxist theory and, more generally, any "phenomenologist" and consciousness-centered approach to psychoanalysis with Lacan as the main interlocutor.

It is thus at this moment around 1963, under the attack of the human sciences, that the existential and phenomenological paradigm, and the figure of Sartre with it, faded into the shadow of structuralism's brilliant glow.

"Anarchical coexistence"

When *The Critique of the Dialectical Reason* came out in 1960 Terray, Badiou, and Verstraeten spent the winter reading it closely. At their request, in April 1961, Sartre gave a lecture on the concept of the possible at the *Ecole Normale*, presenting the theoretical framework of his book in front of Althusser, Canguilhem, Hyppolite, Merleau-Ponty, and students who were present: Badiou, Terray, Verstraeten, Roger Establet, and some of the younger students, Yves Duroux, Etienne Balibar, Pierre Macherey, and Jacques Rancière. According to Althusser,[95] Sartre seemed embarrassed insofar as he simply nodded to questions without giving any direct answers. According to Duroux, this was the "apogee and the end of something"[96] and for Rancière this was Sartre's intellectual "funeral."[97]

This was not Badiou's opinion. Reading *Almagestes*, we find Badiou's implicit commitment at articulating the Sartrean doctrine of freedom as temporal *ek-stasis* together with formal structures, a passion for the literary and political engagement.[98] In this combination of disparate elements, it is not by chance that Badiou chose Ptolemy's famous astronomical treatise as the title of his book.[99]

Badiou will later argue that his generation (with, for instance, Terray, Verstraeten, and Clément) constituted itself in a "mixture of elements,"[100] in an "anarchic coexistence."[101] Later, Badiou will state that he had "formed the project of one day constructing something like a Sartrean thought of mathematics, or of science in general, which Sartre had left aside for the most part."[102] As such, *Almagestes* is a book about language and signs (it uses diverse registers, such as theater writing, mathematical and musical writing, internal monologue, etc.). Here Badiou is far from proclaiming the end of the *book* as Maurice Blanchot[103] had pronounced around the same time, and remained at a distance from the the independence of language as locator, much as the author of the "*nouveau roman*" and the partisans of *Tel Quel* seemed to do. In an interview with Pierre Desgroupes in the television programme "*Lecture pour tous*" in April 1964, Badiou explained that his intention with the trilogy announced in *Almagestes* (*Almagestes*, *Portulans* and *Béstiaires*) was one of reconstructing a "totality," of "once again finding a certain sense of the whole [*tout*]."[104] This would bear the mark of his philosophical upbringing, which could not be but Sartrean.

Badiou's idea was that the crisis of literature had to be solved in a different way than the one proposed by the "*nouveau roman*," namely through a limitation of the range of expressivity. The intention behind the book seems to be political, given the fact that in the last chapter of the book Badiou describes a demonstration where "human violence" disrupts the proliferation of a language called "*Première verité*", a first truth. In fact, in "Saisissement, dessaisie, fidélité," Badiou will later say that the only generic procedure of that time was the political one.[105] The four "witnesses" of this "event" *avant la lettre* are "the subject of scientific Knowledge (for the philosophers, the transcendental subject)," the "social inertia (the serial man)," "esthetic reproduction (image)," and the "beginning of practice."[106] Therefore the "inverse trajectory" would then go from language, intended as the sedimentation of ideology, to history. This is a curious conclusion for someone that, sixteen years later, in *Theory of the Subject*, will claim that "history does not exist" and that "there are only disparate presents whose radiance is measured by their power to unfold a past worthy of them."[107]

Much later, when Badiou reflected on this period, he considered his age to have been an advantage to those "younger" students of Althusser and Lacan, those who did not have the opportunity to be Sartreans. As such, they had missed the opportunity to enter into this question of the subject before its great restructuring through psychoanalysis and structuralism.[108]

On 12 May 1963, the occasion of Jean Hyppolite's election to the *Collège de France*, Badiou sends him a letter[109] which included a manuscript of *Almagestes*. In this letter, Badiou asks Hyppolite when the latter would finally publish the book that he "had promised" to his former students: *Existence et Structure*. We can only imagine that what the former student sought from his professor was a means to keep these "anarchical" elements of structuralism and existentialism together.

Mise en scène

Dina Dreyfus was a curious character, born in Italy, *agrégée* in philosophy, between 1935 and 1938 she participated, with her first husband Claude Lévi-Strauss, in a French cultural mission to Brazil. Though her work as an anthropologist had never been recognized, Dreyfus later become a secondary school teacher and, during the 1960s, the "Inspector General of Philosophy" for the *Academie de Paris*, a job that had been Canguilhem's (1948–55). The job entailed inspecting and setting the agenda for the teaching of philosophy at the secondary school level on a national scale. Dreyfus was a close friend of Canguilhem, who was then the president of the examination committee for the *agrégation*, a professor at the Sorbonne and the director of the Institute for history and philosophy of science. She was also friends with Jean Hyppolite, who was then teaching "history of philosophical thought" at the *Collège de France*, but who had been, from 1954 to 1963, director of the *Ecole Normale Supérieure*. Between Dreyfus, Canguilhem, and Hyppolite, these three people occupied perhaps the most important strategical positions in the French academic world and the administration of public education.

The links between the three allow us to understand the range of participants invited to participate in this pedagogical television series. Serres had been a lecturer at the *Ecole* to help students prepare their *agrégation* exam. Ricœur had been Hyppolite's collegue at the Sorbonne and was, together with Dreyfus and Althusser, part of the "association of the professors of philosophy." Aron was also teaching at the Sorbonne and had studied at the *Ecole* when Hyppolite, Sartre, Canguilhem, Merleau-Ponty, and Nizan were still there. Finally Foucault was a student of both Hyppolite and Canguilhem. No doubt this range of figures showcased the *crème de la crème* of the academic philosophy scene in Paris and provided a Paris-centric, *Ecole Normale*-centric perspective on philosophy. This fully corresponded with the reality of philosophy in France, concentrated around three or four major Parisian institutions: the *Ecole Normale*, the *Collège de France*, the *Sorbonne*, and two or three prestigious preparatory secondary schools where students were trained to pass the entrance exam to the *Ecole*. All the invited philosophers except for Ricœur had been *Normaliens* and almost all of them were invited, at one time or another, by Hyppolite to give talks at the *Ecole Normale*. The youngest of these participants, Serres, Foucault, and Henry, had also been students of Hyppolite and had their doctoral dissertations supervised by him.[110] This impressive cast makes the absence of Gilles Deleuze, Jacques Derrida, and Louis Althusser quite felt. Finally, neither Lévi-Strauss, Roland Barthes, nor Jacques Lacan were participants. This may be due simply to the reason that they were not considered as philosophers and hence in strict terms "outside" the discipline.

La scène

These broadcast interviews could be seen as fulfilling a double role. On the one hand the films aimed at underlining philosophy's peculiarity and distinguishing philosophy from other disciplines, such as sociology, psychology, and anthropology.[111] The attitude, as Jean-Louis Fabiani describes it, was to "guard over the espistemological borders,"[112] insofar as it aimed at allowing philosophy to dialogue with other disciplines while at the same time underlining the philosophical nature of questions that were irreducible to the analysis furnished by natural and social sciences. The history of philosophy, a discipline that since Victor Cousin occupied a central position in the academic system, assured and gave certitude to the continuity and identity of a discipline from Plato to Sartre. Historians of philosophy as different as Martial Gueroult, Ferdinand Alquié, Jean Hyppolite agreed on a number of points: that philosophical texts of the past were not likely to be fully understood without a *philosophical* approach. In this social context, history (as a separate discipline) or psychology were unable to attain a philosophical engagement with these texts, which in turn meant that philosophical thought possessed a tradition and an identity, and that authentic philosophical texts, althought written in the past, possessed something that allowed them to be current and relevant to contemporary problems.

On the other hand, the television broadcasts collected here also aimed to render current philosophical discussion and dialogue accessible to a larger public through the "new" televisual medium.[113] The position of philosophy in the social space in France was very peculiar. Since 1809 philosophy was incorporated in the secondary school curriculum. Philosophy was thought of, in this last year of secondary education, as a "crowning discipline,"[114] the furnishing of a synthesis[115] that would ensure the proper republican education of the citizen. This broad presence of philosophy implied that philosophical texts had a wide reach and that important authors would have to relate to different audiences: secondary school students, university academics, and the "citizens" taking part in the life of the republic.

This is the reason why at the start of each emission there is a short montage of the Latin Quarter. In this pan of bookstores, parks, cafes, and city squares, on buses, the voice-off declares that "philosophy has a life outside our classroom." This "outside" was both conceived as the *"cité idéale"* composed of all the philosophers of all time and the public spaces portrayed by the film. These public spaces were of course the very ones that had been put at the center of attention by Sartre and the existentialist wave. As Tamara Chaplin Matheson writes, the films aimed at showing that "philosophy lives in the wider world, but also, that this world is inimitably French."[116]

Dreyfus, through the televisual medium and through the exposure of the philosopher's bodily presence, wanted to show that philosophy was a linguistic practice,[117] developed by a community of embodied minds, ones in dialogue on film. The director of this project, Jean Flechet, trained at *Institut des Hautes Etudes Cinematographiques*, used several cameras, ones that focused on the faces of the each interlocutor and another that captured the larger setting of the discussion. One might understand also that, as in the round-table "Philosophy and truth," Flechet and

Dreyfus wanted to show the omnipresence of philosophy, showing Hyppolite and Canguilhem discussing on the streets and in the taxi taking them to the *Ecole Normale*.

Television constituted a powerful medium and was able to reach a large audience of secondary school students and even university students or the citizen on the streets. It was for this audience that educational television was established in July 1951 and the *Institut Pedagogique National* (IPN) had disposal of two hours of national airtime each week. In 1963 Christian Fouchet, the minister of education, launched a plan for the development of audiovisual resources and boosted this presence of pedagogical programming to more than fourteen hours a week. This reform was coordinated with the equipping of 6,000 schools with televisions. This series, "*Le Temps des philosophes*," was in fact shown at school in the presence of the teacher.

The potential audience of those films was, therefore, large. After the Second World War, especially during the 1950s, the student population rose exponentially. Badiou recalled that new universities seemed to be opened at the beginning of each month.[118] These films, then, aimed not only at showing that intellectuals were producing philosophical discussions in every corner but that there were questions that depended on a philosophical approach. At the same time, they implicitly demonstrated that any student could in principle have access to, understand, and study philosophy. Of course, the reality behind all of this was quite different. Curiously enough, in 1964, when the films began being shot, Pierre Bourdieu, a young assistant in sociology at the Sorbonne[119], published, with his collegue and friend Jean-Claude Passeron, two books on education: the sociological study *Les étudiants et leurs études* [*The Students and their Studies*],[120] and the *The Inheritors: French Students and Their Relations to Culture*.[121] Both those two books and the later *Reproduction: In Education, Society and Culture*[122] aimed at showing, through statistics, that despite the universal access to education, nothing prevented the actual reproduction of the pre-existent social hierarchies. Along this line, it was during the 1960s that student unions such as the *Union nationale des étudiants de France* (UNEF) and the *Fédération des groupes d'études de lettres* (FGEL) aquired significant power. Yet as Badiou will later comment, the critique of the access to the university and the academic transmission of knowledge was not comparable to the one that accompanied May 1968: what was criticized were the "academic mandarins" and the "old forms" of learning such as the *leçon frontale*. In this, "the dispositif of the *grandes écoles*" remained untouched. The reformers merely asked that the "circle be enlarged" but the hierarchy itself remained completely unchanged.[123] The challenge would eventually be launched during May '68.

Actiones sunt suppositorum

In these blurring currents of intellectual, social, and institutional events, what remains to be commented on is the constitution of a generic voyaging subject, however fictive, that weathered these challenges. Here, like the parallel tidal changes in Anglophone analytic philosophy, French philosophers were equally faced with the constraints imposed by the post-war educational and social context, the paradoxes of the hard sciences that challenged their given philosophical assumptions, and the emerging prominence and rigorousness of the social sciences, the linguistic turn, and the increasingly difficult question of the relevance of philosophy to modern life. In this current, we can point to many of this French generation like Jean-Claude Milner, who introduced Chomsky's linguistics to a whole generation of French students, and Jacques Bouveresse, who championed analytic philosophy through Wittgenstein and Quine in France. As such, this collection of interviews is also a representation of the last period where French philosophy, as *French* and as *philosophy*, could still afford to be effortlessly endogamic. That is, with the emerging tide of the urge for philosophy and philosophers to become "theoretic" with regard to political engagement, an all-or-nothing affair of completely immersing one's reading of, say, Spinoza, to Marxist-Leninist terminology, or *not*, and the philosophical engagement with the Anglophone tendency to submit the status of knowledge entirely to post-classical physics, modern mathematics, the innovations of linguistics, anthropology, and sociology. The philosophers interviewed here could still maintain a certain distance to this twin trend, against the notion of *theory* on one hand and against serving as the handmaiden to science on the other. In this, Aron, in his interview, remarks that one should know *something* about sociology and Canguilhem, who assigns truth to science, poses an ultimately introspective attitude toward science through the terms of the essence of science or a reflexive treatment of sciences that will deeply differ from the more positivistic approach to "practice" of science or the path of the Marxist "science" of historical materialism. We note here that Sartre's model of engagement, one that Badiou still held on to in this period, is not like the sort that followed. Neither philosophy nor the philosopher will so comfortably pronounce itself in this voice of essence. Rather what we see emerging in the late 1960s is the opening of philosophy to politics and modern science where philosophy saw itself "sutured," to borrow one of Badiou's later expressions borrowed from Miller, to these domains in such as a way that it gives up its privilege of autonomy except in the most nominal way.[124]

In this, Badiou could be held up as a transitional figure. We cannot fail to note that immediately after the period of these interviews, Badiou wrote and published, under the promotion of Althusser, "The Concept of Model," a treatment of model theory that would become for a number of years a significant philosophical introduction to formal logic, surprisingly peppered with Althusserian expositions and the characteristic notions of Badiou's eventual systematic philosophy. This is consistent with the general opening up of French philosophy against both the hegemonic position of philosophy through the cornerstone of "history" with regard to other disciplines and also with regard to a new orientation, one that understood itself as the theoretical component to a practice that could only be concrete with respect to society and politics. It was in this vein that Badiou, after 1968, would continue in the "anarchic" elements of two different paths. He rejected the hegemonic position of the philosopher in the model of Bergson and Sartre by opening philosophy to the technical developments of logic and mathematics. At the same time, Badiou arrives at this through the transformation into a politically engaged *theorist*, with a certain suspicion of philosophy, in the style of Althusser. Speaking comfortably in the voice of philosophy today, much of this transformation towards an engagement in both science and politics still remains perhaps paradoxical. As such, Badiou is known equally well as an ontologist of Zermelo-Frankel set theory and Grothendieck Topoi as well as the unrepentant Maoist through his polemic *Circonstances* series and his punctual contributions to *Le Monde*.

In this sequence of events however, we should not let ourselves be carried away in reading these developments into this earlier sequence. This volume cannot represent these movements whether in Badiou's own development of the larger transformation of the French institution of philosophy but only represent a still moment at the start of these transitions. If we stick solely with Badiou as an allegorical figure of a larger transformation, it is in this still frame that we will trace some of the ideas that will eventually characterize his mature thought. For brevity's sake, we point to three moments.

As a first moment, we identify a problematic that had perhaps reached its zenith in Badiou's higher education years. This is the question of the relation between truth and science. The persistence of this theme in French philosophy has for a background the twin figures of the Neo-Kantian Leon Brunschvicg and Vitalist Henri Bergson who very much provided the twin *foci* of the French philosophical orbit during the early twentieth century. In the period leading up the Second World War, this underlying theme was brought to bear on increasingly concrete and precise quandaries by the chemist-turned-philosopher Gaston Bachelard and the mathematican-philosopher Jean Cavaillès. Much of what gave the identity of *academic* French philosophy leading up to this period of the early 60s was this powerful trend of engaging with science while maintaining the borders of philosophy. This was of course complicated by the rise of the social sciences and the dialogue that it took up with philosophy. The philosophical skepticism toward whether the social sciences could properly be called "science" and whether its knowledge is on par with those of biology or even physics is of course something that remains a current in French philosophy today. But the importance of Lévi-Strauss' polemics with Jean-Paul Sartre in his 1962 *The Savage Mind* can be seen as the moment of fracture where what was revealed was philosophy's blunt naiveté concerning matters of the human world. While the former "epistemological" trend tied to the "hard sciences" would soon wane after the late 1960s, the influence of the social sciences would become more and more marked not only in the structuralist legacy but the outgrowth of sociology represented by figures like Pierre Bourdieu, who was also later interviewed as part of the television series not reproduced here.[125]

In all this, the intimacy of the status of truth to science was already a constant feature at least in the form of a question in French philosophy at this time. In Badiou's work, this question will eventually transform into a theory of conditions where four domains, science, art, love, and politics, rather than philosophy, will be understood as the productive and constructive sources of truth. As we see, at least as it concerns science, Badiou puts up no resistance to Canguilhem's strong insistence of this strict identity between truth and science. Of course Canguilhem will go on to assert that the strict identification of science with truth does not forbid other forms of value to concern us *qua* humanity.[126] In this, philosophy, at least along this view, is the mediator where one reflects on the essence of scientific truth and brings this into relation with a totality of other social and human concerns.[127] Bracketing the more traditional parlance of "values" posed by Canguilhem, Badiou's mature theory of conditions, where philosophy establishes itself by coordinating and rendering "compossible"[128] different domains of truth from the combination of science, art, politics, and love, is not ultimately that far off from the view expressed by Canguilhem here. This is of course not to say that it is the same. Badiou's eventual development of this position occurred in the late 1980s in the full swing of deconstruction, post-structuralism and post-modernism. In this era of post-modernism and "science studies," science was strictly analyzed as a practice without any real regard for its content, the facts that it was aiming to establish. Truth, on the other hand, was treated purely as a claim of truth, useful only in understanding an empty place that material and social forces sought to localize within a discipline regardless of whether one was dealing with, say, physics or sociology. Of course the implication of all this social construction and relativity with regard to scientific truth reinstated a certain sovereignty of philosophy, a meta-discourse capable of giving "meaning" to all these social and discursive phenomena. Going through the trials of post-modernist fire, Badiou's revival of this epistemological legacy is indeed old-fashioned and one that directly refers back to this period where Canguilhem still lectured from his podium at the Sorbonne.

Secondly, just when the relation of truth and science was being contested, the problem of historicism, a major legacy of the French Neo-Kantians as well as the Hegelians, was a major question of the day. As one of the leading Hegel scholars and translators of his day, there is no question that Jean Hyppolite would have been asked to pronounce on this issue. Badiou's relationship with Hyppolite was close and this was the director with whom Badiou would have done his doctoral thesis. Regardless, the temporality of truth has been a major issue in philosophy at least since Heraclitus and the historicity of philosophy was no small feature in any part of Aristotle's writings. In this period, after the Neo-Kantians, the Hegelians and the singular influence of Heidegger, it was not only a problem that philosophers made their pronouncements according to their historical constraints. The persisting problem was the evolution and temporal localization of truth itself. Badiou's unique response to the question through the notion of the event, a pronouncement of truth that is at once historically local and eternal in its process of becoming, borrows heavily from Hegelian dialectic (and the Hegelian notion of reason) but also owes itself to the subtraction of truth from philosophy. This unique response detailed in the 1988 *Being and Event* may be seen as a simple combination of entrenched Hegelianism, a dash of Heideggerianism and a compromise with post-structuralist critique.

Yet viewed from this perspective of the early 1960s this result was no decided matter. Badiou's eventual theory of truth as both localization and eternity employs the indiscernible and undecidable nature of this truth. Here Badiou's use of these two terms "undecidable" and "indiscernible" will be largely borrowed from the development of the completeness proofs in set theory. That is, Badiou will base his paradigm of truth, not only on mathematics, but also on the history of the paradoxes and problematics of mathematics in the twentieth century. This is of course in direct opposition to the distinction that Hyppolite makes in his interview with Badiou. The very first thing that Hyppolite says is that the history of philosophy and the history of science, and in particular mathematics, is none other than the fact that philosophy carries with it its own historical past, conceived and reconceived at each epoch. In Hyppolite's view, this is not the case for mathematics (or science in general) where results and facts at their present stage are the only issues that are on the table. If we believe Badiou, it was through the work of Albert Lautman[129] that he came to his mature view concerning the status of mathematics, one that would eventually lead him to the mathematical ontology of *Being and Event*.

In his exchange with Hyppolite however, we see one side of this deeply historical concern for both the eternity and temporality of truth. The moment that this concern finds a root in Badiou's full-fledged transfer of truth toward science (and the other conditions), the dialectic of the temporality and eternity of truth slides along with this movement into the "conditions" themselves, whether in science, politics, love, or art. Philosophy, in turn, becomes the ahistorical outside of its instantiation in personal lives *qua* biographies.[130] As such, while Hyppolite saw the inertia of the history of philosophical problems and transformations as weighing on philosophy today, Badiou will encounter an open space where concepts are never extinguished but brought into newer formations with respect to the truths of their time, constellated around the truth conditions. In turn, it is truth itself, now localized in the various conditions like politics and mathematics, that will bear the burden of their immediate history, their paradoxes, and their unrealized capacity. This is something of an inversed Hegelianism but one that was already put to question in this early period in dialogue with Hyppolite.

The third moment of contrast and comparison has to do with ethics. This reference is made to the most peculiar of the interviews collected here, the exchange with Michel Henry. As we see in the interview, it is Badiou that does most of the talking and Henry strangely plays the part of the Socratic interlocutor. Here we find Badiou going a bit off-script by negating the importance of the question of ethics altogether. This is of course what Badiou will do in his 1998 book *L'éthique*.[131] In this book, translated as *Ethics*, Badiou reencounters a familiar terrain. This text was solicited as a secondary school level book and the editor, Benoît Chantre, imposed those same restrictions against technicality, against verbosity and a relation with current affairs that must have reminded Badiou of those days where he conducted these interviews under the guidance of Dina Dreyfus. In this book, just as in those interviews, Badiou launched a full-out attack on the very idea of an ethics that would be, as we are familiar today, an underlying code for behavior, a deontological prescription, an aim toward the moral whether conceived as Aristotelian excellence or Hellenistic happiness. The mature Badiou will have a good reason for denying these claims for an ethics and a morality. For this mature figure, what is of importance is the idea of justice such as was interrogated by Socrates. In such a claim, the necessarily indeterminate nature of justice is one that takes on a historic shape through the figure of the subject and not, as he lays out in *The Century*[132] as well in *Ethics*, something that can be approached directly as personal responsibility, human virtue, or even as the abstract notion of "obligation" that ethicists speak of. If we wish to speak of a constant between these interviews in the early 1960s and Badiou's eventual development, it is on this point that we find a constant. In his exchange with Henry, we find an unrelenting interpretation of "ethics" as "morals" in the ideological sense. That is, one feels obligated to do something or behave in a certain way because of the surrounding subjective formation of the role that we are called to play. Whether as mother, doctor, or legislator, the range of actions given to these roles do not exist in the void but are assigned according to social constraints to which motivation, worth, and responsibility is assigned. Although Badiou was not yet at this moment inscribed into the Althusserian circle, we can see much of Althusser's 1969 text "Ideology and Ideological State Apparatus" in this general movement.[133]

Badiou's presentation here not only shows a part of the philosophical context in which this strong move toward ideological analysis was received but also shows his own skepticism of philosophical discourse about general or universal ethics. That is, ethics are themselves engendered in particular practices or through particular roles which are in turn traceable, in the precedent set down by Nietzsche, to a genealogy of "morals." This localization of ethics, in the mature Badiou, of course does not mean that they are inherently relative. As we remarked earlier, truth can emerge eternal despite their temporal and geographical localization. The difference between ethical practice within ideological confines and those that attain universal status is due to the context of the event. This evental context is of course both exceptional and unpredictable. As such, within Badiou's mature context, an ethical act is either caught within the limited confines of an ideologically constrained field or an undecidable dimension where there is no reducible "moral" content of action.

Across these three moments, we can trace continuity and distinction. One could both be enticed by the underdetermined links of transition in Badiou's work and just as easily be swept away in the currents of influence in French philosophy. Against Badiou's habit now of saying – alluding to Bergson – that "a philosopher only has one idea,"[134] we might retort that not only does an idea make its own trajectory but that a philosopher certainly makes a voyage along a number of different coasts.

§§§

In Badiou's elegy to Borreil with which we began, he notes that an interrogation is not exactly a thought but a movement of thought that sets sail towards an uncertain future. What we have attempted to capture above and in this volume is a setting sail, with Badiou as interrogator, but not from the perspective of a salty sea dog who spins a fantastic yarn of his adventures. Rather, we read off the well-marked sailor's log where the registration of coordinates and ports of call designated what would have been a destination.

In 1964, Alain Badiou, a secondary school teacher in provincial Reims was called back to the capital to participate, with the most established philosophers of the French intellectual context, in a philosophical television series that would be broadcasted to a new generation of students sitting for the *Baccalauréat* exam. This simple fact does not allow us to say that either this participation or this televisual project as a whole caused what was about to happen in France, nor did it determine Badiou's future philosophical trajectory. This absence of causal determination does not however forbid us from grasping a voyage on solid ground.

Notes

1   Alain Badiou, *Pocket Pantheon: Figures of Postwar Philosophy*, trans. by David Macey (London: Verso, 2009), 147–8.

2   Francois Cusset, *French Theory*, trans. by Jeff Fort (Minneapolis: University of Minnesota Press, 2008).

3   The New Philosophers [*nouveaux philosophes*] is a term which refers to a generation of French philosophers who broke with Marxism in the early 1970s and who promoted themselves as media personalities. The group included André Glucksmann, Alain Finkielkraut, and Bernard-Henri Lévy. They pretended, in the name of democracy and anti-totalitarianism, to criticize Jean-Paul Sartre and "post-structuralist" thinkers such as Deleuze or Badiou, as well as the philosophy of Friedrich Nietzsche and Martin Heidegger.

They were in turn attacked by critics such as Gilles Deleuze (who called them "TV buffoons"), Pierre Vidal-Naquet, Alain Badiou, Jean-François Lyotard, and Cornelius Castoriadis.

4   Interview between Alain Badiou and Frédéric Taddéï in the radio show "*Le Tête-à-tête*" broadcasted through *Frence Culture* on 11 December 2011.

5   Alain Badiou, "Almagestes," in *Les Temps modernes*, 19, 212 (January 1964). Three years later Badiou will publish in the same journal an excerpt from *Portulans*. Alain Badiou, "L'autorisation," in *Les Temps modernes*, 23, 258 (1967). Apparently De Beauvoir will later take from *Almagestes* the character of the "mole" that she used in her 1966 novel *Les Belles Images*. Cf. De Beauvoir's interview with Jacqueline Piatier, "Simone de Beauvoir présente *Les Belle Images*," in *Le Monde*, 23 December 1966, 17.

6   Televised interview between Alain Badiou and Pierre Desgroupes, "*Lecture pour tous*," first broadcasted on 22 April 1964. Looking at this interview, we might also conjecture that, outside of his intellectual talent, Badiou was selected by Dreyfus for the job as interlocutor because of his ease in front of the camera.

7   Sartre considered Almagestes as a book which puts questions in "the most radical and intransigent manner." Cf. "Jean-Paul Sartre s'explique sur *Les Mots*," interview with Jacqueline Piatier, in *Le Monde*, 18 April 1964. This interview translated by Anthony Hartley as "A Long, Bitter, Sweet madeness" in *Encounter*, 22, 6 (June 1964): 62.

8   "Sevriénne" was a student of the *Ecole Normale Supérieure des Sèvres*, the female counter-part to the *Ecole Normale Supérieure* which would only become co-educational in 1985.

9   Cathérine Clément, *Mémoire* (Paris: Flammarion, 2011), 129. Cf. Cathérine Clément, *La putain du diable* (Paris: Flammarion, 1996), 59–60. Badiou will use Gracq's novel *The Opposing Shore* to explain his theory of "points" in *Logics of Worlds*. Cf. Julien Gracq, *The Opposing Shore*, trans. by R. Howard (London: Harvill, 1997). Cf. Alain Badiou, *Logics of Worlds*, trans. by Alberto Toscano (London: Continuum, 2011).

10   Cf. Alain Badiou in interview with Francois Gauvin, "Les mathématiques sont la seule discipline capable d'expliquer l'être," online, *Le Point*, 4 April 2011, http://www.lepoint.fr/grands-entretiens/badiou-les-mathematiques-sont-la-seule-discipline-capable-d-expliquer-l-etre-04–04–2011–1314877_326.php accessed 20 April 2012.

11 Jean Delsarte entered the *Ecole Normale* in 1922, d'Henri Cartan, Jean Coulomb and René de Possel in 1923, Jean Dieudonné and Charles Ehresmann in 1924, Claude Chevalley in 1926.

12 Cf. Marc Heurgon, *Histoire du PSU* (Paris: la Découverte, 1994).

13 Cf. Alain Badiou in interview with Peter Hallward on 6 May 2007, "D'une Théorie de la structure à une théorie du sujet," website for the *Cahiers pour l'analyse* project, http://cahiers.kingston.ac.uk/ interviews/badiou.html accessed 15 April 2012.

14 Cf. Alain Badiou in interview with Frédéric Taddéï in the radio show "Le Tête-à-tête," cit.

15 Simone De Beauvoir, "Merleau-Ponty et le pseudo-Sartrisme," in *Les Temps modernes* 10, 114–15 (June 1955): 2072–122. Translated as "Merleau-Ponty and Pseudo-Sartreanism," by Veronique Zaytzeff and Frederick Morrison in *International Studies in Philosophy* 21 (1989): 3–48.

16 Cf. Alain Badiou in interview with Christine Goémé, "Le bon plaisir," on *France Culture* first broadcasted on 11 November 1995.

17 The four characters were probably inspired respectively by Pierre Verstraeten, Emmanuel Terray, Badiou himself, and his wife Françoise.

18 See for example the discussion about desire and psychoanalysis. Alain Badiou, *Almagestes*, (Paris: Seuil, 1964), 60–1.

19 "Given that consciousness is a projection in the world, no box can represent it, *exterior* monologue." Alain Badiou, *Almagestes*, 49n.

20 Jean-Paul Sartre, *Being and Nothingness*, trans. by Hazel E. Barnes (New York: Grammercy Books, 1956), lxii.

21 Badiou, "Saisissement, *dessaisie, fidélité,*" Les Temps modernes, 46 (October 1990): 14.

22 Badiou, "Saisissement, *dessaisie, fidélité,*" 14.

23 For an assesment of Badiou's relation with Sartre throughout his intellectual trajectory, see Patrice Vermeren, "Alain Badiou, fiel lector de Sartre 1965/2005 (Collages)," in *Jean-Paul Sartre, Actualidad de un Pensamiento*, ed. by Horacio Gonzalez (Buenos Aires: Ediciones Colihue, 2006), 7–22. See also Emmanuel Terray, "Badiou et Sartre," in *Autour de Badiou*, ed. by Emmanuel Terray (Paris: Germina 2011).

24 See the footnote 11 of a review Badiou wrote of *Reading Capital* and *For Marx*, "Le (re)commencement du matérialisme dialectique," where he defends Sartre against the attacks of Althusser who treated Sartre as a "philosophically dead"

idealist who "does not teach anything." Alain Badiou, "Le (re) commencement du matérialisme dialectique," *Critique*, 240 (1966): 444–5. Cf. Louis Althusser, "The Philosophical Conjuncture and Marxist theoretical research," in *The Humanist Controversy and Other Writings*, trans. by G. M. Goshgarian (London: Verso, 2003), 1–18.

25   Alain Badiou, "Hegel in France," in *The Rational Kernel of the Hegelian Dialectic*, ed. and trans. by Tzuchien Tho (Melbourne: Re. Press, 2011), 14.

26   "In truth we only become a philosopher by being, first, the disciple of someone. I do not think there is another real becoming other than first being a disciple of somone." Alain Badiou in interview with Christine Goémé, "Le bon plasir," cit.

27   Alain Badiou, "Le cinéma m'a beaucoup donné," in *Cinéma* (Paris: Nova editions, 2010), 13–40.

28   Emmanual Jalley remembers that this was a journal "full of good intentions" to which those who were invited to contribute were "all the students of the institutions considered the most talented." Emmanuel Jalley, *La guerre des psys continue: La psychanalyse française en lutte* (Paris: Harmattan, 2007), 403.

29   Alain Badiou, "La comédie du mensonge," *Vin nouveau* 1: 4–13.

30   Alain Badiou, "Voyage à Bayreuth," in *Vin nouveau* 13: 68–72.

31   Alain Badiou, "La culture cinématographique," in *Vin nouveau* 5: 3–22. This text has been published in the collection *Cinéma*. Badiou, *Cinema*, 41–62. In the dialogue placed as an introduction to this recent volume, "Le cinema m'a beaucoup donné," Badiou notes that he was, like many in that period, an enthusiast of cinema. In the present volume, we include a retrospective text, "The critical value of images," where Badiou underlines this very importance, in films as well as in television, of "presence." In this article in *Vin nouveau*, Badiou, following Sartre, defines cinema as an "art, namely a presence of the human being in the significations given in the world" and attributes the importance of cinema's capacity of describing "temporalized psychological states." Badiou, "Le cinema m'a beaucoup donné," 15. Part of Badiou's analysis here was probably inspired by Merleau-Ponty's 1945 essay "Cinema and New Psychology." Cf. Maurice Merleau-Ponty, "Cinema and New Psychology," in *Sense and Non-Sense*, trans. by Hubert Dreyfus and Patricia Allen Dreyfus (Evanston: Northwestern University Press, 1964).

32   Alain Badiou, "La poèsie de Senghor," *Vin nouveau*, 103: 67–79.

In this article Badiou also makes mention of Sartre's interest in *"negritude."* Senghor apparently sent Badiou a letter a few weeks after the publication of this article. Cf. Jacques Louis Hymans, *Léopold Sédar Senghor: an intellectual biography* (Edinburgh: Edinburgh University Press, 1971), 80.

33 Alain Badiou, "Présence de l'SFIO," *Vin nouveau*, 3: 48–50. This article was first published in *Flèches: Bulletin des étudiants socialistes des écoles normales* in January of 1957.

34 The *'talas'* was the nickname for Catholic students at the *Ecole Normale*.

35 Collective authorship, "Urgence pour Algérie," in *Vin nouveau*, 8: 3–7.

36 The last chapter of *Almagestes*, "Première vérité," is a description of one of these demonstrations.

37 Cf. Alain Badiou, Emmanuel Terray, et al., *Contribution au problème de la construction d'un parti marxiste-léniniste de type nouveau* (Paris: François Maspero, 1970).

38 These political activities and others are reported in *Almagestes*.

39 In the interview "Les mathématiques sont la seule discipline capable d'expliquer l'être," Badiou explicitly says that "under the influence of Sartre and hostile to colonial wars, I became a militant. May 1968 and its consequences radicalized this engagement." Alain Badiou, "Les mathématiques sont la seule discipline capable d'expliquer l'être," cit.

40 For a sociological enquiry on the journal's position, see Anna Boschetti, *The Intellectual Enterprise: Sartre and Les Temps Modernes*, trans. by Richard C. McCleary (Evanston, IL: Northwestern University Press, 1988).

41 See the August-September 1953 issue of *Les Temps modernes* especially Jean Pouillon essay, "D'une politique de négation au néant d'une politique." Cf. Jean Pouillon, "D'une politique de négation au néant d'une politique," in *Les Temps modernes*, 93–4 (August 1953): 425–46.

42 Jean Cohen and Mohamed Chérif Sahli, "L'Algérie n'est pas la France," Les *Temps modernes*, 11, *119* (November 1955): 577–615.

43 English translation in *Interventions: international journal of postcolonial studies*, 3, 1, 1 (March 2001): 127–40.

44 See on this point his conference "Vous etes formidables," *Les Temps modernes*, 135 (1957) reprinted in Jean-Paul Sartre, *Situations V* (Paris: Gallimard, 1964): 57–67.

45   Louis Althusser, *The Future Lasts Forever*, ed. by Olivier Corpet and Yann Moulier-Boutang, trans. by Richard Veasey (New York: The New Press, 1993), 329.

46   Cf. Edward Baring, *The Young Derrida and French Philosophy 1945–1968* (Cambridge: Cambridge University Press, 2011).

47   Cf. Jean-François Sirinelli, "Les Normaliens de la rue d'Ulm après 1945: une génération communiste?," *Revue d'histoire moderne et contemporaine*, 33, 4 (1986): 569–88.

48   Alain Badiou and Bruno Bosteels, "Can Change be Thought?," in *Badiou and politics* (Durham: Duke University Press, 2011), 294.

49   Claude Lévi-Strauss, "Des indiens et leur ethnographe," *Les Temps modernes*, 11, 116 (1955): 1–50.

50   See Pierre Nora, "Préface" to Claude Lévi-Strauss, *Tristes tropiques* (Paris: France Loisirs, 1990). Cf. François Dosse, "Le moment ethnologique dans la culture française," *Le Débat*, 5, 147 (2007): 100–11.

51   Cf. Badiou, "D'une Théorie de la structure à une théorie du sujet," cit.

52   For his conversion to anthropology, see Jean-Paul Colleyn and Emmanuel Terray, *Traversées. Livres, actions, voyages* (Bruxelles: Labor, 2005), 76. In *Le Marxisme devant les sociétés primitives*, Terray thanks Badiou for his help in the writing of "Morgan et l'anthropologie contemporaine." Cf. Emmanuel Terray, *Le Marxisme devant les sociétés primitives* (Maspero: Paris 1969).

53   Pierre Verstraeten, "Lévi-Strauss ou la tentation du néant," *Les Temps modernes*, 19, 206: 66–109; *Les Temps modernes* 19, 207: 507–52. This essay is dedicated to Badiou.

54   Claude Lévi-Strauss, *The Elementary Structures of Kinship*, trans. by J. H. Bell, et al. (Boston: Beacon Press, 1969).

55   The only recorded publication by Françoise Badiou, who later become a sculptor, is "Formules d'inversion de Möbius." Cf. Françoise Badiou, Théorie des nombres in Charles Pisot, Hubert Delange, Georges Poitou (eds), Seminar in number theory: 1960–1961 (Paris: secrétariat mathématique, 1962). Françoise probably inspired the character of Chantal in *Almagestes*, who is evidently a mathematician. She declares: "I love mathematical writing. It is flexible, it resembles those long blades of grass that one finds in the mountains." Alain Badiou, *Almagestes*, 103.

56   Matieu, born in 1934, was a mathematician but he slowly abandoned mathematics for painting. See Badiou's and Pierre

Verstraeten's essays in the collection of essays *Posthume sur mesure*. Maurice Matieu, *Posthume sur mesure* (Paris: Regard, 2007). Matieu's paintings can be found in some of the books of Badiou's and Cassin's collection '*L'ordre philosophique*'. He is also mentioned in *Almagestes*, 107.

57 Suzanne Bachelard, *La conscience de rationalité. Étude phénoménologique sur la physique mathématique* (Paris: PUF, 1958); *A Study of Husserl's Formal and Transcendental Logic*, trans. by Lester Embree (Evanston, IL: Northwestern University Press, 1968).

58 Gilles-Gaston Granger, *Pensée formelle et sciences de l'homme* (Paris: Aubier, 1960).

59 Jules Vuillemin, *Philosophy de L'Algebre* (Paris: PUF, 1962).

60 Jules Vuillemin, "Le problème phénoménologique: intentionalité et réflexion, " *Revue Philosophique de la France et de l'Étranger*, 149 (1959): 463–70.

61 Edmund Husserl, *L'Origine de la géométrie* (Paris: PUF, 1962).

62 Jean Cavaillès, *Philosophie mathématique*, ed. by Roger Martin (Paris, PUF: 1962).

63 In a review of Gueroult's posthoumous book *Dianoematique*, his pupil Victor Goldschmit writes that the term technology, often used by Gueroult, "designates the study of *demonstrative structures* proper to each system" [emphasis added]. Victor Goldschmit, "Dianoématique," in *Ecrits: Etudes de philosophie moderne* (Paris: Vrin, 1984), 229.

64 Althusser eventually created this seminar to which Badiou contributed in 1967.

65 They will furnish the material for his *Spinoza. Dieu (Ethique I)*. Martial Gueroult, *Spinoza. Dieu (Ethique I)* (Paris: Aubier-Montaigne, 1968).

66 Cf. Gilles-Gaston Granger, "Jean Cavaillès ou la montée vers Spinoza," *Les Etudes philosophiques*, 2 (July 1947): 271–9.

67 According to François Regnault, Canguilhem was often talking about Cavaillès and about this book, that he edited, in his lectures about logics. Cf. François Regnault in interview with Peter Hallward on 1 May 2008, "Tout d'un coup, la psychanalyse: un entretien avec François Regnault," website for the *Cahiers pour l'analyse* project, http://cahiers.kingston.ac.uk/interviews/regnault.htm accessed 15 April 2012. Apparently Canguilhem used to couple Spinoza and Cavaillès and had been

director of Yves Duroux' DES thesis on Cavaillès and Pierre Macheray's DES thesis on Spinoza.

68 See Terray, "Badiou et Sartre," but also a recent essay by Badiou echoes his DES thesis "What is a proof in Spinoza's Ethics?". Cf. Alain Badiou, "What is a proof in Spinoza's Ethics?", in *Spinoza Now*, ed. by Dimitris Vardoulakis (Minneapolis: Minnesota University Press, 2012), 39–49.

69 Roland Barthes, *Writing Degree Zero*, trans. by Annette Lavers and Colin Smith (London: Jonathan Cape, 1967), 79–82.

70 Roland Barthes, *Mythologies*, trans. by Annette Lavers (London: Paladin, 1972).

71 For these aspects see Anne Simonin, "La mise à l'épreuve du nouveau roman. Six cent cinquante fiches de lecture d'Alain Robbe-Grillet (1955–1959)," *Annales. Histoire, Sciences Sociales*, 55, 2 (2000): 415–37.

72 Phillipe Sollers, "Tel Quel, " in *Théorie d'Ensemble* (Paris: Seuil, 1968), 392.

73 "D'une Théorie de la structure à une théorie du sujet," cit.

74 "D'une Théorie de la structure à une théorie du sujet," cit.

75 See interview with Jean Hyppolite in Dominique Janicaud, *Heidegger en France*, Vol. 2. (Paris: Albin Michel, 2001), 68. Cf. Alain Badiou's talk on Hyppolite at the *Ecole Normale* in 2005 now published in the collection *Pocket Pantheon: Figures of Postwar Philosophy*. Here Badiou reports that in 1959 he gave Hyppolite a first manuscript of *Almagestes* and that Hyppolite recognized some of his Hegelian reflections about the Greeks in a dialogue. Cf. Alain Badiou, Pocket Pantheon, 44–5. In fact, one of the characters in *Almagestes* says: "When I was in Greece, my dear, I understood the Temple [...] We found in the earth and in the stone the inverse meaning of human labour. All of Marxism." Alain Badiou, *Almagestes*,229.

76 See Emmanuel Jalley, *La psychanalyse française en lutte*, 393.

77 See Alain Badiou in interview, "Le bon plaisir," cit.

78 Alain Badiou in interview, "Le Tête-à-tête," cit.

79 See Emmanuel Jalley, *La psychanalyse française en lutte*, 394.

80 Edward Baring, *The Young Derrida and French Philosophy*, 100–1.

81 This text was published few months before in the 1958 issue of *L'Evolution psychiatrique*. Jean Laplanche, "A la recherche des principes d'une psychothérapie des psychoses," in *L'Evolution*

psychiatrique, 23, 2 (1958): 377–8. In *Almagestes*, in a dialogue between two characters, one of which seemed to be inspired by Hyppolite, Badiou evokes this essay: "the unconscious is a salad, it's better to call it bad faith [...] In fact, have you read the last article, in *Intellect*, on the psychosis? Very strange. A structuralism...." Alain Badiou, *Almagestes*, 230.

82   See "D'une Théorie de la structure à une théorie du sujet," cit.

83   Daniel Lagache, *L'Unité de la psychologie* (Paris: PUF, 2004).

84   We can find the rejection of this sort of psychology in a dialogue of *Almagestes* when the character of Dastaing, the political activist, proclaims "throw Bergson in the toilet" [*aux chiottes Bergson*]. Badiou, *Almagestes*, 166.

85   This is what Badiou will call the "right wing" criticism of the notion of subject. See Alain Badiou, *Logics of Worlds*, 522.

86   This was a talk given at the *Collège de Philosophie* in 1956. Georges Canguilhem, "What is psychology?," trans. by Howard Davies, *Ideology and Consciousness*, 7 (1980): 37–50. A transcription of the talk was also published in 1958 in the journal *Revue de la metaphysique et la morale* and later in 1966 in *Cahiers pour l'analyse*. Georges Canguilhem, "Qu'est-ce que la psychologie?," *Revue de la metaphysique et la morale*, 1 (1958): 12–25; *Cahiers pour l'analyse*, 2 (February 1966): 75–91. Canguilhem also gave a series of seminars on history of psychology at the Sorbonne in 1959–60.

87   Emmanuel Jalley, *La psychanalyse française en lutte*, p. 398.

88   In the interview "D'une Théorie de la structure à une théorie du sujet," Badiou admits that during that period Althusser "was not active" and that "he was very often absent."

89   This will end in the publication of Pierre Macheray's article, "La Philosophie de la science de Georges Canguilhem: Épistémologie et histoire des sciences," in the 1964 issue of *La Pensée*, later collected in Macherey's edited publication in 2009. See Pierre Macherey, *De Canguilhem à Foucault. La force des normes* (Paris: La Fabrique, 2009).

90   See "D'une Théorie de la structure à une théorie du sujet."

91   Claude Lefort, "L'échange et la lutte des hommes," published in 1951 in *Les Temps modernes* and later included in the collection *Les Formes de l'histoire*. Claude Lefort, *Les Formes de l'histoire*, (Paris: Gallimard, 2000).

92   Jean Pouillon, "L'œuvre de Lévi-Strauss," published in 1956 in *Les*

Temps modernes and later published under the title "L'invariant et la différence." Cf. Jean Pouillon, "L'invariant et la différence," in *Fétiches sans fétichisme* (Paris: Maspero, 1975).

93   Paul Ricœur, *The Symbolism of Evil*, trans. by Emerson Buchanan (New York: Harper and Row, 1969).

94   Cf. Jean Laplanche and Serge Leclaire, "The Unconscious: A Psychoanalytic Study," trans. by Patrick Coleman, *Yale French Studies* 48 (1972): 118–75.

95   Althusser mentions this episode in *The Future Lasts Forever*, 337–8.

96   See Yves Duroux in interview with Peter Hallward on 7 May 2007, "Structuralisme fort, sujet faible: un entretien avec Yves Duroux," in website for the *Cahiers pour l'analyse* project, http://cahiers. kingston.ac.uk/interviews/duroux.html accessed 15 April 2012.

97   See Jacques Rancière in interview with Peter Hallward on 2 May 2008, "Que sous forme de la rupture: un entretien avec Jacques Rancière," in website for the *Cahiers pour l'analyse* project, http:// cahiers.kingston.ac.uk/interviews/ranciere.html accessed 15 April 2012.

98   The only mention of structuralism in the book, in a dialogue between two characters, is followed by a critical remark by one of them, who treats the structuralist position of the other as a "pataphysics of the linguistic field." Badiou, *Almagestes*, 61.

99   The title comes from a verse of Saint-John Perse's poem *Exile* that Badiou uses as an epigraph. It is not by chance that on the back cover of the issue of *Vin nouveau* in which Badiou published his first essay (November 1956) we find these same lines from the poem *Vents* by Saint-John Perse: "Et ne voyez-vous pas, soudain, que tout nous vient à bas – toute la mature et tout, le gréement avec la vergue, et toute la voile à même entre visage – comme un grand pan de croyance morte, comme un grand pan de robe vaine et de membrane fausse. Et qu'il est temps enfin de prendre la hache sur le pont?" [And do you not see, suddenly, that everything is crashing around us – all the masting and everything, the rigging with the main yard, and the whole sail over our faces – like a great fold of dead faith, like great folds of empty robes and false membranes. And that at last, on deck, it is time to use the axe?] Saint-John Perse, *Winds*, trans. by Hugh Chisholm (New York: Pantheon Books, 1961), 37. The title of the second novel by Badiou is also inspired by the poems of Saint-John Perse relating to the theme of sea voyages. The title *Portulans: trajectoire inverse* is an explicit

reference to the "Portolan charts" which were were navigational maps, first made in the 13th century in Italy and later in Spain, based on compass directions and estimated distances observed by the navigators at sea.

100 See "D'une Théorie de la structure à une théorie du sujet," cit.

101 Alain Badiou, "Saisissement, dessaisie, fidelité," 16–17.

102 See Alain Badiou and Bruno Bosteels, "Can Change be Thought?," 295.

103 In 1964 Badiou sent Blanchot a copy of *Almagestes* with the following dedication: "to Maurice Blanchot – witness of the keeping of silences."

104 Alain Badiou, "Lecture pour tous," cit.

105 Badiou, "Saisissement, *dessaisie, fidélité*," 14.

106 Badiou, *Almagestes*, 311.

107 Cf. Badiou, *Logics of worlds*, 509.

108 Alain Badiou and Bruno Bosteels, "Can Change be Thought?," 294.

109 Alain Badiou, unpublished 1963 letter to Jean Hyppolite in the Hyppolite archives at the *Ecole Normale Supérieure*.

110 Hyppolite supervised Foucault's introduction and translation of Kant's *Anthropologie du point de vue pragmatique*, Serres' *Le système de Leibniz et ses modèles mathématiques*, and Henry's *L'Essence de la manifestation*.

111 Dreyfus was determined to defend philosophy against all attacks coming from the social sciences, as she states clearly in an article she co-authored with Florence Khodoss and that was published at the same moment. Dina Dreyfus, "L'enseignement philosophique," in *Les Temps modernes*, 235 (December 1965): 1001–47.

112 See Jean-Louis Fabiani, *Les philosophes de la République* (Paris: Minuit, 1988), 97.

113 For these aspects and the social analysis of the films see Tamara Chaplin Matheson, "Embodying the Mind, Producing the Nation: Philosophy on French Television," *Journal of the History of Ideas*, 67, 2 (April 2006): 315–41.

114 See Jean-Louis Fabiani, "La discipline de couronnement," in *Les philosophes de la République*, 49.

115 For this aspect see Jean-Louis Fabiani, *Les philosophes de la Répubique* and *Qu'est-ce qu'un philosophe français?*. Jean-Louis Fabiani, *Qu'est-ce qu'un philosophe français? La vie sociale des concepts (1880–1980)* (Paris: EHESS editions, 2010).

116 Cf. Tamara Chaplin Matheson, "Embodying the Mind, Producing the Nation."

117 See, on this point, the short essay by Alain Badiou, "The critical value of images," included in this volume. Alain Badiou, infra.

118 "D'une Théorie de la structure à une théorie du sujet," cit.

119 In 1966, Bourdieu participated, with Jean Laplanche, Georges Mounin, Jean Hyppolite, and Dina Dreyfus in a series of three episodes on "Philosophy and Language" in the same series.

120 Pierre Bourdieu and Jean-Claude Passeron, *Les étudiants et leurs études* (Paris: Mouton, 1964).

121 Pierre Bourdieu and Jean-Claude Passeron, *The Inheritors: French Students and Their Relations to Culture*, trans. by Richard Nice (Chicago and London: University of Chicago Press, 1979).

122 Pierre Bourdieu and Jean-Claude Passeron, *Reproduction: In Education, Society and Culture*, trans. by Richard Nice (London: Sage, 1990).

123 Alain Badiou, "D'une Théorie de la structure à une théorie du sujet," cit.

124 Cf. Alain Badiou, *Manifesto for Philosophy*, trans. and ed. by Norman Madarasz (Albany: SUNY Press, 1999), 61.

125 Pierre Bourdieu along with Jean-Claude Passeron will eventually be interviewed in the same televised series in 1967 in two different emissions under the titles "Sociologie et sociologie spontanée" and "Vigilance épistémologique et pratique sociologique."

126 Cf. "Philosophy and science," infra.

127 Cf. "Philosophy and truth," infra.

128 In Badiou's mature work, notably in his *Manifesto for Philosophy*, he uses the Leibnizian term *compossibility* to designate the contemporaneous coordination of truths. Cf. Badiou, *Manifesto for Philosophy*, 43.

129 Cf. Alain Badiou, "Custos Quid Noctis," *Critique* 450 (November 1984): 861.

130 For Badiou's own understanding of his philosophy as a biographical trajectory see Alain Badiou, *Philosophy as Biography*, in *lacan.com*, 13 November 2007, http://www.lacan.com/symptom9_articles/badiou19.html accessed on 23 January 2010.

131 Cf. Alain Badiou, *Ethics*, trans. by Peter Hallward (London: Verso, 2002).

132 Cf. Alain Badiou, *The Century*, trans. by Alberto Toscano
     (Cambridge: Polity Press, 2007).

133 Cf. Louis Althusser, "Ideology and Ideological State Apparatuses,"
     in *Lenin and Philosophy and Other Essays*, trans. by Ben Brewster
     (New York: Monthly Review Press, 1971).

134 Alain Badiou in interview with Tzuchien Tho in *The Concept of
     Model*, ed. and trans. by Zachary Luke Fraser and Tzuchien Tho
     (Melbourne: Re. Press, 2007), 102.

CHAPTER ONE

Philosophy and its history

Jean Hyppolite and Alain Badiou

First broadcast: 9 January 1965

Alain Badiou: Jean Hyppolite, I would like to start by asking the following question: Why is there a history of philosophy and what is the specificity of this history?

Jean Hyppolite: Well, I think we can't, at least not today, philosophize without the history of philosophy,[1] that is, the history of the great philosophical works and the great systems of the past. When you want to initiate someone into philosophy, since you are a philosophy teacher as I am, you need to put them in contact with the philosophers of the past. This is exactly as if one wanted to learn poetry, there is only one way: read the poets. Only that this history does not resemble, for example, the history of mathematics, which dissolves into contemporary mathematics, for example we know how the imaginary number was established, we know this because we understand certain structures today and, in brief, the history of mathematicians and of mathematics is nothing but a series of anecdotes in relation to a foundation which is completely current. We cannot take up all the philosophers of the past and somehow reduce them into a current philosophy which would forget succession in order to maintain a history of repetition.

AB: On this point, should we conclude that philosophy is closer to poetry, for example, than mathematics?

JH: What interests mathematicians is the rigor of form. This is a formalism that has nothing to do with what the philosophers sometimes call form: philosophers also want to prove, philosophers also want rigor. Yet mathematicians attain a formal system, a systematicity. A system of philosophy will never arrive at this even if the organization of a work, the way in which it links up its evidence, is fundamental. However, with the poet, for I have not responded for the poet, with the poet, this is what we have in common: the aim of the poet is also not mathematical formalism but something different. The aim of the poet is the beautiful and the aim of the philosophy is the truth.[2]

AB: This history of philosophy, which is neither the history of the beauty of systems, nor the anecdotal history of philosophers, I suppose … [JH: surely not!] What is it then finally?

JH: Well, it is, one needs to add, neither the history of scientists nor the history of science. It is not the history of science, it is different. We need to assert that philosophy exists. This first point means, for us, doesn't it, that philosophers exist: Plato, Descartes, Spinoza, Leibniz, Kant, are philosophers.

AB: But then there are philosophers such as Malebranche who reject the importance of history of philosophy, and those like Hegel, who absorb it and ends up being dissolved in it. Is it not already to make an affirmation of a type of philosophy to say, as you do, to first state the necessity of the history of philosophy?

JH: I think that all philosophy that we know, in the end, since the philosophy of the Pre-socratics until our philosophy, until Kant, marks an irreversible movement. It flows in an irreversible direction, just like time, just like filled time, like a full time, and this irreversibility makes it such that philosophy is a question for itself, metaphysics is a question for itself. Since Kant, in particular, something occurred and which makes it such that metaphysics has without doubt become: what is metaphysics? It is no longer a question of doing metaphysics, a theory of being or a theology, it is a question of asking what this metaphysics is, and in what measure it is possible.[3]

AB: But this question of critique is it not, in some respects, the announcement of the end of philosophy?[4]

JH: An end … of metaphysics?

AB: And maybe even of philosophy?

JH: Ah! For the salt of the earth that would be lost! You know quite well! […] Simply put, if you like, the metaphysicians of the past worked at a theory of being and in general they also worked at a theology. It is this theology that is not our question today, this does not mean that the problem of being, the problem of metaphysics itself has ceased, has been accomplished. This perhaps means that a system such as that of Spinoza or a system such as … Descartes, who was not that systematic but even a system like that of Descartes is impossible today even though we absolutely have the need to read Descartes and Spinoza in order to do philosophy.

AB: But even so I would like to ask you about the nature of this need. If the question itself, or rather a formulation of the philosophical question has been modified, if it means the possibility of a metaphysics and not on the possibility of constructing a metaphysical system, we can ask ourselves what is the properly philosophical interest of studying the Pre-critical authors, after all?

JH: That's it! Should we begin philosophy with Kant and not to go all the way back to Plato, for example?

AB: This seems to me a bit of what results from what you say.

JH: It is perhaps difficult to understand what I am saying. I mean to say that the philosophical systems of the past represent a first degree of thinking, if I dare say. This is not thinking itself but gives us a sort of existent metaphysical thinking with this double character and this double character is the link between a matter and a form. I mean the thought of a philosopher is a thought that wants to think being, that wants to think content, unlike mathematical thought, for example, and it is at the same time a thinking that wants to be rigorous and not arbitrary. For them, the knowledge of knowledge and the knowledge of being are coupled together. Simply put, the philosopher of the past does not pose this question of its possibility, or at least, it is only posed implicitly. We are the ones who unearth these latent questions today in these philosophers.

AB: I will summarize a bit of what you have said and I may end up caricaturing it a little. Philosophy is a project of thinking being in the current terms of its becoming and has become the thinking of this thinking, that is to say, the attempt to give a foundation, in a critical manner, the very possibility of a thinking of being. This movement is basically, for you, the very movement of the history of philosophy. So I would like to ask again, in sum, a question that I have already asked: is this history in a sense that would not be purely metaphorical or analogical? What is actually historical about this history?

JH: You have summarized my thinking in a way that I do not accept, when you say to me (but maybe I really did said this after all!) that we went from the thinking of being to the thinking of the thinking of being. Is this what you said?

AB: Yes ...

JH: This would mean that current philosophy is a purely critical philosophy which examines thoughts which are thoughts of being but that no longer aims to reach being, and absolutely no longer aims to reach content.

AB: Yet you were the one who said that that the question "What is metaphysics?" was at the basis of the fundamental question of all contemporary philosophy.

JH: Yes, I said that we need to put metaphysics itself into question but this does not mean that the question of being was abandoned. Simply put, the question of being and the thinking of being is perhaps no longer posed in philosophy in the way that it was done by Malebranche, for example, or even like it was posed by Descartes, but this does not mean that the philosopher stops being one who, from the starting point of existence, starting from her existence in her own time, reaches for being in a certain way. Simply put, one no longer thinks being as if God would be the idea of being, it is thought from the position of the human being and from anthropologically existential roots, through a human being which is not cut off from being. But this thinking of being clearly no longer corresponds to the ambition of creating a theory like those of the great metaphysicians. I am not sure that Plato ... you know, we have taken him to be a skeptic in different moments in history, someone who did not err, but who wandered, who touched on questions, who doubted, and for whom thinking could not be identified with a system like those we mentioned a moment ago, but instead a sort of philosophical inquiry.

AB: Since the intention that animates the earlier systems of philosophy are now according to you impracticable, would you accept us speaking of an error in these systems? Or an error in these philosophers?

JH: No, I would not employ the word "error." I do not use the word "error" because of what interests us a philosophical system. When we contemplate a system of philosophy, it is the path taken by the philosopher, it is the manner in which she gains access to truth, and it is also the way that she touches it [truth] of course! This occurs in such a way that I would nonetheless concede something. I would concede to you that in what concerns metaphysics as such, all that we might want from metaphysics, we might say that something has been overcome, in a certain way, that history has put it into question. But in what concerns the interior of the system, it seems to me too general to speak of an error at the interior of a philosophical system. It seems to me, if you like, difficult, for example, to take a whole class of philosophers and say:

"There we go! Descartes was mistaken about doubt." Or, "Descartes was mistaken about this or that ..." I do not think that a philosopher is refuted by another philosopher, even if they take themselves to be refuting one another, I do not think that the refutation of a philosopher by another philosopher is something that makes much sense.

AB: So for example, concerning Descartes, yes – you cited him! – what would you draw from him?

JH: Listen, I draw two things: as you know, he is a great philosopher and his thought represents a system. A system that has an order of reasons,[5] isn't it, through which thinking is made coherent, shows what our means of understanding are and what we grasp when we reach understanding? I draw from Descartes the total thought of Descartes, the Cartesian oeuvre, the thought that is carried with it. There is also the weight of his thought in what would follow in [the history of] metaphysics, in the philosophical and historical succession. Cartesian doubt, maybe he did not doubt enough – you can tell me if I am going to reproach him – but Cartesian doubt is a movement that one always needs to take up.

AB: Would you accept [this approach] in cases where assertions appear paradoxical or even scandalous, I am thinking of – I don't know – the theoretical justification of slavery by Aristotle, to take a banal example. Would you say that, in this case, what is in question is precisely the existential rootedness of the problematic that you just evoked?

JH: Surely! Surely! A philosophical thought has its existential roots. And what I understand by this is that it is rooted in its time and in its epoch even if its aim, its perspective, is not exactly of this existential perspective. Plato sought to save the Greek city-state in the moment where it was disappearing. In fact, he did not succeed in saving it! ... and what he did was what Hegel called "the rose in the cross of the present."[6] He produced a thought that seemed to be eternal and was taken by many to be so; and nonetheless we know very well that his thought also belonged to a moment in history. The philosopher thinks her time, and surely it is difficult to cut philosophy off from its existential roots.

AB: But in this case, would philosophy not have its truth in the non-philosophical?

JH: Or would the non-philosophical not have its truth in philosophy? I respond a little too simply, a little too dialectically, but why would you want that ... this really ends up saying that philosophy is nothing but ideology ...

AB: ... for example ...

JH: ... in an epoch. But this is what I generally refuse. I do not want to confound philosophical thought with ideology. I think that there is a strict relation between philosophy and the non-philosophical, between philosophy and its conditions, between philosophy and the conditions of its time; the philosopher thinks her time, she was raised in thought and she depends on non-philosophy to the degree that – we can recall what I said to you about mathematical formalism – to the degree that it is not a pure form and to the degree that there are non-philosophical sources of philosophy ...

AB: But, but ...

JH: There are sources which are not philosophical. But if you permit, we have spoken a great deal about systems, don't think that I exclude the philosophy of the great skeptics or of the great empiricists who did not have systems. I mention this so as to avoid giving the idea that I consider philosophy to only be systems.

AB: My worry is not so much to contest the conception of the history of philosophy that you have proposed to us but much more of asking if the word history is not rather equivocal. That is whether there is not a mere resemblance between the history of the historians and a philosophical history of philosophy such as you have just described it here due simply to the use of this very word, the word history.

JH: I think I would concede to you everything that you are saying at this moment. In saying that the history of philosophy is different, we mean that the word history does not have just one meaning. But first the history of philosophy is like the other [kinds of history] because one needs to look at sources, one needs to analyze the language, one needs to analyze a thought, but only in order to understand it. Would you say to someone, even in literature, is it really enough to analyze all the conditions of a text, of a great text, should one not also find its beauty, its aesthetic sense?

AB: That is exactly right, exactly, but you go further ...

JH: Yes.

AB: ... you do not say that philosophical truth is the affair of philosophy. That would be nothing but a banality just as if one says that the beauty of the work is the affair of aesthetics. You seem to mean that the very history of philosophy, that is, philosophy as becoming and not only as truth is the affair of the philosopher and not the historian. Here, I am not sure that your example is adequate, for the history of art is an historical discipline.

JH: Beauty does not seem to me to be opposed to the pluralism of beautiful works, there could be the beauty of Shakespeare which is not contradictory even if it is quite different from the Greek tragedies. You agree with me on this ...

AB: Yes ... yes.

JH: ... on this point. Yet there is something that bothers us when we speak of two contradictory philosophical systems that are both true. It seems that there could only be one truth ...

AB: Right, on this problem ...

JH: ... I was the one who said that but ... so the truth of being is such that it renders possible – as I think has been said by the historians of philosophy like Gueroult, for example – that nature, the essence of being and reality are such that opposed points of views be held on this same being.[7] Whether they logically follow or whether there is a becoming, I don't know … you asked me a question that … there is certainly a historicity, I told you at the beginning of this conversation that I think the history of philosophy cannot treat philosophers through the sort of eternal perspective with which the history of mathematics treats mathematicians. There is thus a succession and thus there is the emergence of philosophical systems, an incontestable historicity but … the nature of being should be such that it renders this diversity or even this opposition between philosophical systems possible.

AB: Since you refuse the existential rooting of philosophy in the mode of ideology, could we perhaps define the meaning of this term? I think that you would not accept us calling you a Marxist.

JH: I wouldn't deny that there is a relation between certain philosophies, the relations of production and the technical conditions of production.

AB: Is it up to philosophy itself to think this relation?

JH: Certainly. It should be thought today. When a philosophy fails to think its own sources – and it never completely thinks it – as I said a moment ago metaphysics is put into question today, I think that a philosopher should not fail to interrogate these very conditions of thinking and the sources that feed into thought which are perhaps religious sources, economic sources, technical sources. Today we are in a time of putting the relationship between the sources and the philosophical thought into question.

AB: This brings me to ask a purely pedagogical question, or at least something seemingly pedagogical – what use according to you can one make of the history of philosophy in your teaching of philosophy and in the classroom?

JH: Yes, not in the teaching of the undergraduate or graduate level of philosophy, yes, the admirable thing that is the secondary school course in philosophy and which I hope remains ...

AB: We all hope so ...

JH: ... but also to adapt to this new world, I don't want to say that the teaching of philosophy should adapt but I mean that the participation of everyone including scientists to what philosophy can contribute to what is liberal and open seems indispensable to me. So the philosophy course should not only be addressed to students in the so-called humanities, but addressed to everyone, to those who will become engineers, scientists and ... there could be an open year in philosophy for everyone [*année liberale en philosophie*].[8]

But coming back to your question of the role of the history of philosophy in the philosophy classroom, speaking strictly in terms of the course; there is what needs to be kept out and what we look for. I think that we can be very categorical in what we keep out. We need to exclude a sort of "textbook" approach to the history of philosophy that does not put students in contact with the great texts or philosophers but gives only a summary of [philosophical] systems from the Pre-socratic up to Kant and Fichte, Schelling and Hegel. We need to exclude this and we also need to exclude the sort of eclecticism that consists in laying out great philosophical questions – empiricism, rationalism and all the "isms" – and to find a median solution. Alas there is still much of this in many of the ways in which we work with students of philosophy. That is, to try to oppose one thesis against another and then combining them. No. In its place, I think it is essential to place students in direct contact with one or two great philosophical works. Naturally we should try to do as many as possible; this would be the best, but I think it is impossible with too many. And if one has to choose just one, I would clearly choose Plato for reasons that would take too long to explain here.

The second important thing is that the philosophy teacher helps students understand that the history of philosophy is not like other histories, it is not a purely empirical history. Philosophy touches something that is of a different order. Students should be allowed to see the uniqueness of the history of philosophy and be put in a direct contact with one or two great philosophers; this is what I expect from the history of philosophy in a philosophy course.

AB: You said a moment ago that you would chose Plato and that you had some very complicated reasons, could you nonetheless explain some of the reasons for this choice.

JH: Well, first there is no Platonic system even though there is systematic thinking. There is an investigation and even a path of this investigation. With Plato we also find a deep connection between him, his epoch and with human life. For example, we spoke a moment ago about the wish to save the Greek city-state even if the feeling was that this was in a state of decline. But there is something stronger as well. At the end of the seventh book, I think, that is in the seventh book of the *Republic*, Plato compares an actual man, or Socrates in Plato's words, compares an actual man to a child who did not know the conditions of its birth ... that its parents were not its real parents and who discovered one day that the people who raised it were not its real parents. A human being is a bit like this, one no longer obeys traditions and customs and needs to search for ways to behave through reason and reason alone. This search is not a solution, no solution was given by Plato. This path of seeking and this opening up of a search is something that attracts me. Just as in all of Plato's thought, I think that there is some manner of bringing these young philosophers to reflect on philosophy.

Notes

1 The history of philosophy, conceived as a discipline reserved to philosophers and related to the practice of philosophy, occupied a central role both in secondary education and academia in France, at least since the 1830s, due to the influence of Victor Cousin (1792–1867). During the 1950s more than half of the chairs at the Sorbonne were reserved to the history of philosophy. From the end of the nineteenth century until the 1950s many debates concerned the epistemological status of the history of philosophy and the peculiarity of philosophical temporality in opposition to the temporality of

scientific. The last of these debates was launched by Ferdinand Alquié (1906–85) who defended the human dimension of philosophical creation, and Martial Gueroult (1912–76) who dedicated his work solely to the analysis of the architectonic of philosophical systems. Most of the teachers with French academia defended the originality of philosophy, the existence of an eternal truth, and an actualizable core of great philosophical texts against the attempts of reducing them to sociological, economic, or psychological causes.

2 These themes, especially the discussion of the relation between philosophical concepts and mathematical formalism on the one hand and between philosophical intuition and poetry on the other had been treated, in relation with Hegel, in Hyppolite's *Logic and Existence*. We point to the third chapter, "Philosophical Dialectic, Poetry, and Mathematical Symbolism." Cf. Jean Hyppolite, *Logique et existence* (Paris: PUF, 1953); *Logic and Existence*, trans. by Leonard Lawlor and Amit Sen (Albany: SUNY Press, 1997).

3 The use of "theology" here is related to a religious context and to the philosophical treatment of the nature and existence of the absolute. It aims however at a distinction between metaphysical and theological (onto-theological) questions. Outside of Heidegger's distinction between these two themes within the history of philosophy, within this context, we point to Pierre Aubenque's separation of metaphysics and theology within Aristotle's *Metaphysics*. Cf. Pierre Aubenque, *Le problème de l'être chez Aristote* (Paris: PUF, 1962).

4 This question is an allusion to Kant's idea of the end of metaphysics and to Heidegger's idea of the end of philosophy. Cf. Martin Heidegger, "Letter on Humanism," in *Basic Writings*, ed. by David Farrell Krell (San Francisco: Harper Collins Publishers, 1993), 213–66.

5 Here, as before, Hyppolite alludes to Martial Gueroult's interpretation of Descartes as a systematic philosopher expressed in his book *Descartes selon l'ordre des raisons*, where the question of the "order of reasons" comes to the fore as a method of reading. Martial Gueroult, *Descartes selon l'ordre des raisons* (Paris: PUF, 1954).

6 This expression is used by Hegel in his preface to the *Elements of the Philosophy of Right* to designate the concrete universal.

7 Jean Hyppolite seems to refer here to Gueroult's idea of a "*réel philosophique*" (philosophical real) to which different philosophical systems can refer. This idea, expressed in the second volume of his posthumously published book on the philosophy of the history of philosophy, entitled *Dianoématique*, was implicitly present in all

of Gueroult's studies in the history of philosophy since the 1950s. Martial Gueroult, *Dianoématique* (Paris: Aubier-Montaigne, 1979).

8 In the French educational system, students spend the last year of their secondary education preparing for the *Baccalauréat* exam. Those who sit for *Baccalauréat littéraire* receive philosophy training but those who sit for the *Scientifique* do not.

CHAPTER TWO

Philosophy and science

Georges Canguilhem and Alain Badiou

First broadcast: 23 January 1965

Alain Badiou: When we speak of the philosophy of science, what should we understand by this? Is epistemology the same thing as the philosophy of science?

Georges Canguilhem: The "philosophy of science" was a positivist term employed by Auguste Comte in the preface of his *Course on Positive Philosophy*. This is the positivist equivalent to "*Wissenschaftslehre*" in the German theory of science or what we later called the "theory of knowledge."

With Auguste Comte, the philosophy of science had the objective of unifying knowledge at least through its method. The objective was that of unification. Precisely because it was unifying, it progressively appeared impossible to accomplish and the very limitation of the scope of positivist philosophy did nothing but confirm that the philosophy of science would eventually degenerate into generalities, that is, first as futilities then finally as banalities.

With respect to epistemology, as opposed to the philosophy

of science, we have a specific and regional discipline.[1] It is the critical study of principles, methods, and results of a science. This critique includes as such an evaluation of results with respect to their methods, and methods with respect to their principles.

Epistemology is thus a study that aims to grasp the history of science that concerns it and can either limit itself to [this scope] or – but this is not without its dangers – extend into a theory of knowledge.

AB: In what sense should we understand the concept of science when we speak of a philosophy of science? That is to say, are there one or many concepts of science? Should we say: science or the sciences?

GC: In any case, the first response is that it is not for philosophy to fix the extension of the concept of science. And when [philosophy] cannot fix the extension [of science], it cannot define its comprehension. The second response is that the concept of science is not univocal.[2]

We cannot say that mathematics and animal physiology are sciences in the same way by the identity of method and immediate aims.

It is only right that I should remark that, on the one hand, there are sciences which are totally formal like mathematics and, on the other hand, there are experimental sciences. So the difficulty is that at some moment the formal serves the experimental for its advancement and that the experimental advances more often through the formal rather than the experimental itself.[3]

It is not up to philosophy to fix in advance the extension of the concept of science. It is not up to [philosophy] to say, at a given moment, that such and such an inquiry, according to some consecrated formula: *sub scientia non cadit.*

However this misadventure happens quite often in philosophy. Let us take an example. There are some scientific disciplines today that are of the highest importance such as astrophysics, astrochemistry and at the other pole: biophysics and biochemistry. These sorts of sciences had no place in some of the classification of the sciences developed by philosophers in the nineteenth century.

In turn, if we cannot fix the extension of science, it goes without saying that it is always risky to define comprehension. This does not mean that we can never speak of science in the singular. We can speak of science in the singular as a phenomenon of culture. Thus science should be understood as theory but in opposition to the other forms of activity and the other modes of human culture.

In recent times we cannot but be struck by the difficulty of giving a definition that convenes univocally on mathematics, and above all modern mathematics, the rigorous science of logic, the science of the intelligibility, and the sciences that we should continue to call experimental, which are the sciences of evidence and the science of the verifiable.

The difficulty is still more acute when we notice that between the sciences that seem to be defined, on the one hand by rigor and on the other by their effectiveness, the relation is such that mathematical theory is very often that which stimulates progress in experimental science.

AB: Do you not think that this difficulty is one of admitting, at the same time, the impossibility of fixing comprehension and the extension of the concept of science and also to argue that a differential comprehension of science is possible in the sum of human practices? Perhaps my question is not very clear.

GC: It embarrasses me. But it is not because it is not clear but because I am myself not clear. I mean to say that incontestably there is a mathematical science today which seems to have developed itself in full freedom. We lay out objects, conventions, and then we see what we can conclude. On the other side, there are people who use complicated tools in laboratories such as electron microscopes and they are those whom I call the experimenters.

This prevents us from proposing a comprehensive definition [of science] that univocally applies to Bourbaki[4] and the Cancer institute. But I think nonetheless that in both cases, it is not the work that we should focus on. This is what I wanted to explain by saying that science should be understood as theory, as an activity that aims to understand through causes or through laws. It is in opposition to another form of activity which is not cut off and separated from precedent. It is very different in terms of its intellectual attitude relative to its object.

AB: Should we continue to radically oppose scientific knowledge and vulgar knowledge?

GC: Yes, more and more. There is no scientific knowledge without, on the one hand, a very elaborate mathematical theory and without, on the other hand, the use of more and more complex instruments. I would even go further to say that there is no such thing as vulgar knowledge.[5]

AB: Should we understand you here as saying that the expression "scientific knowledge" is pleonastic?

GC: You understand me perfectly correctly. This is what I mean. Knowledge that is not scientific is not knowledge. I would hold that "true knowledge" is pleonastic as well as "scientific knowledge"; "science and truth" as well. These amount to the same thing. This does not mean that there is no aim for the human mind outside of truth or that there is no value outside of truth, but this means that you cannot call knowledge what it is not and you cannot articulate it in a way that has nothing to do with truth, that is outside of rigor.

There is either truth in the formal sense or truth in the sense of the coherence in the interpretation of phenomena. There is no other.

AB: What does it mean then, when we speak of a vulgar knowledge?

GC: We mean, for example, either perception which is no knowledge at all or the rules of empirical technique, the contents of the expression such as "a bird in the hand is worth two in the bush," etc.

Vulgar "knowledge" is the vulgarization of knowledge that might have been considered scientific in the past and which constitutes a routine, technical traditions, etc.

Gaston Bachelard gave, in this respect, a remarkable example. According to vulgar knowledge, an electric light bulb burns when it is lit up. Scientific knowledge of an incandescent light bulb consists in understanding that it does not burn in the vulgar sense. That is to say, a vacuum has been created in the bulb that prevents combustion.

AB: Is there a general object in science like matter, nature, world, or universe?

GC: I respond negatively. None of these terms appears to have a correctly explainable meaning. That is to say that I don't see what can be defined in itself as the object of science whether it be matter, nature, world, or universe.

AB: Should we continue to distinguish between a purely theoretical, disinterested research and practical applications of science?

GC: I think that we should continue to distinguish between theory or what we call fundamental science today and the applied sciences which are not yet, it seems to me, [the domain of] applied technology. To say that we need to distinguish between these, at the same time, in terms of object and method, does not mean that we can separate them.

AB: You have given, I believe, lessons on the origin and the history of technology.[6] Could you tell us what we should understand by technology?

GC: We should not use "origins" since these are not origins, these are commencements. Origins were with the Greeks. For us, we began in the eighteenth century, that is to say in the commencement of modern technology.

Here I would give an overview of what we have done during the year. We did not do historical research except in the domain of bibliography and we have looked at works but we have not entered into the archives. In France everyone speaks of technology without always knowing what it is. Everyone says that we should talk about it in school. Yet there is no one capable of speaking for an hour on this issue. It is actually quite difficult.

I now respond directly to the question. "Technology" is a Greek word that means the presentation of the rules of an art.

The Romans borrowed it and for a long time, we might say until the seventeenth century, it was held as equivalent to rhetoric and grammar.

In the eighteenth century, in this traditional definition, "art" becomes once again technical and took up the following meaning: operation of using natural forces or primary materials to economic ends.

Technology is what in the eighteenth century, in France, the *Academy of Sciences* and the Encyclopedists called the description of industrial arts [*arts et métiers*]. But the term "*technologie*" did not exist in French at this time. The French term was borrowed from the Germans and was introduced into France at the end, we could even say at the end of the eighteenth century, by Cuvier,[7] born in Montbéliard, who studied in the Caroline Academy in Stuttgart. It was Cuvier, the secretary of the institute, who introduced the term "*technologie.*"

The reports of Cuvier on the progress of science that were published at the beginning of the nineteenth century all contained a section on "technology."

We need to explain how the Germans came to this term "technology." We considered with reason that it was employed for the first time, "*technologie*" in German, in 1777 by Johannes Beckmann, born in 1739 and died in 1811, who occupied the first research chair dedicated to technology in Göttingen. The Germans claim to have created the thing, the form, and the name. In reality, they did not create the name, this was transported from Latin into German, and if they had created, in the academic sense of the term, the thing, they only responded to a wish that was already formulated by Leibniz at the end of the *New Essays.*[8] In all these cases, the first, to my knowledge, that used "*technologie*" – in Latin "*technologia*" – in the strict sense of the sciences of the arts and the products of art, was the famous Leibnizian philosopher Christian Wolff, in his *Preliminary Discourse on Philosophy in General* of 1728 on the classification of philosophy. He used the expression "*technologia scienta artium et operum artis,*"[9] the science of art and the products of art, and by "products of art" he specified that one needs to understand this as (and this shows the difference of the meaning of the term employed up until that time) the works of the organs of the body and more precisely one's hands.

And thus Wolff gave a name to a wish formulated on the last page of the *New Essays on Human Understanding*.

The work of Beckmann, published in 1777, had the title [in French translation]: *Introduction à la technologie ou à la connaissance des métiers ; des fabriques et des manufactures* [Introduction to technology or the knowledge of crafts, workshops and manufacturing plants].

In short, at the same time a well delimited concept, as an ordinary term, and as an academic institution, technology has a German origin in the second half of the eighteenth century.[10]

AB: Is the history of science part of science or of the philosophy of science?

GC: The history of science is not part of anything; this is a problem of pedagogical destination and academic localization. We need to distinguish the difference of situation outside and inside France.

In foreign countries: in Germany, in Anglo-Saxon countries and in the Soviet Union, it is usually done and taught by scientists who do the history of science either complementarily or when they are not doing their own scientific work.

In France, more often than not, the history of science was written by philosophers and this is one of the effects of the influence of the positivism of the nineteenth century. But there are also examples of the history of science written by scientists. I bring up the names of Paul Tannery,[11] Pierre Duhem,[12] and René Dugas[13] and as a recent example the *Elements of the History of Mathematics* by the team of mathematicians under the name Bourbaki.

AB: You have opposed or at least compared a history of science undertaken by scientists and a history of science undertaken by philosophers. Is there not a worry precisely that the history of science by scientists would exclusively be the history of truth such that appears to them in their practice, whereas the history of science of philosophers would be envisioned as, or perhaps more so, a history of errors?

GC: I don't see why there wouldn't be two sorts of histories of

science because effectively what is done by scientists is trans-
parent and liquid understood in the sense that the time of
this history flows fluidly. For the philosophers, it is opaque
and viscous. Only we find that there are points of technique
in the history of science that cannot be well studied or well
presented except by scientists. The idea should be, in sum,
that of cooperation or collaboration. But philosophers, when
they do the history of sciences, are too lofty to address the
documentary information provided by these histories undertaken by scientists.

In any case, when a philosopher provides the objective of the
history of science they should not provide a certain vague ideal
or of generality.

Reciprocally, the histories of science undertaken by the scientists in the United States, in England, and in Germany are not
necessarily histories of great periods that aim at representing an
evolution. It is often one of erudition. This history of science
undertaken by scientists is very particular and very scholarly and
even if it is not of a philosophical vastness or penetration, it has
merit in its exactitude.

AB: You do not see a hierarchy between these two [forms of]
history, but rather a complementarity?

GC: I see quite a complementarity. Very often I know that a scien-
tist's history turns toward a collection of anecdotes, but it also
happens quite often that a philosopher's history turns toward
apologetics.

AB: What is philosophical in the history of science?

GC: What is philosophical in the history of science concerns its
indirect relationship with science and not through the fact that
it is directly historical. Science is the search for truth. This search
has engendered extravagances, aberrations, missteps, and [thus]
necessarily [also] rectifications.

So in science as such, that is to say as an activity that
cannot be followed without self-reflection to some degree, the
mind certainly aims at something that it doesn't really know.
The history of science – and Bachelard has taught us this in

an eminent way – is a history of evaluation and not only of description.

For example it is because there was, in the eighteenth century, the birth of modern chemistry that a history of alchemy becomes interesting, fascinating even, [but] in a certain sense scientifically useless. In speaking strictly of the history of sciences, it is the history of past knowledge that had future [effects].

But we must prevent, starting from the perspective of the history of sciences, a substitution of a philosophy of the history of science for a philosophy of sciences which I said a moment ago is impossible today. One must not identify the future of a science in the past with the future of a science to come.

As such, since the history of sciences cannot strictly be descriptive and since it should never be anecdotal, it is always philosophical to some degree. But I repeat, this does not mean that we should only or that we could only have a philosophy of the history of science.

AB: Concerning the traditional problem of the value of science, even though it has ceased being part of the official curriculum [*programmes officials*], does it have any relevance today?

GC: I think that it is not without reason that the question has disappeared from official programs. Science is today justified in itself through its value – if by value we understand its capacity to apprehend reality –since it has reached a point of transformation. It is possible that the problem of the value of science is still relevant today but in the form of a misunderstanding. Under the expression "value of science" people understand: what should we hope for in the atomic age?

AB: You measure the value of science in its power to apprehend the real and you measure its power for apprehending the real in its power to transform it. This power of transforming the real, does it belong, according to you, in science properly speaking or in its application?

GC: It belongs clearly in its application but it is precisely in its application that it gives proof that explication is not purely verbal.

AB: In a sense is it thus not false to say that the value of science is in technique?

GC: Your question risks replaying the misunderstanding that I alluded to in my response to that question.

Let's clear one thing up: technique as application constitutes the value of science as explication. This is the same reason why a laboratory experimentation constitutes the proof of the validity of a hypothesis. In a certain sense there is no separation between a university laboratory and an industrial test center except from the perspective of methods or techniques.

AB: Can we say that there is truth in the sciences?

GC: If we don't speak of the truth in sciences then where and of what do we speak about? In my sense, there is only one domain that we can speak of truth and this is in science.

AB: You have said that we can only speak of truth, in all rigor, in the order of science. Would it be indiscreet to ask what for you signifies reality in philosophy, if there is no philosophical truth?

GC: There is no philosophical truth. Philosophy is not a science and in turn I think that the term truth is not suitable for it: that does not mean that philosophy is a game without [its own] stakes. The value of philosophy is in something other than truth.

Truth is not the only value that is established by human beings. This does not mean that philosophy is any less than science. Philosophy [occurs when] science is confronted with other values that are foreign to it, for example aesthetic and moral values.

It is this confrontation with the presumption that the term is a concrete unity that seems to me the object of philosophy. It is difficult for me to say what legitimates philosophy but it is probably not its success, understood in the common sense of the term as the adequacy of its project with its result. It is not in its success since this adequacy is never obtained.

AB: What do you understand by truth insofar as you recognize it in science and not in philosophy? Outside of success, is there not a coherence within philosophy?

GC: Philosophical coherence and scientific coherence are not of the same nature. Scientific coherence is a coherence at the interior of certain conventions, or a coherence at the interior of certain rules of the determination of an object. In philosophy there is no convention and there is no specific object.

There is no convention for philosophy in the way that there is in mathematics; in philosophy there is no limited object.[14] This is unlike optics or macro-molecular biochemistry. Philosophy is a project that concerns a totality.[15] Philosophy cannot be less than science, we need it to conserve scientific [truth] but it encircles it, only implicitly, because it makes use of certain results, the coherence that renders these results possible. When philosophy integrates these results they cannot be treated as if they were obtained by a method other than what took place. We need to take them as true but as true in order to do something else. This "something else" that can be made of [science] should not be called the true, just as we cannot say that it is the good.

Philosophical value is not truth value. Further, it is also not the value of freedom as in morality or aesthetics. This is an idea of an all where each of the values would have its place relative to others. But in this moment we need to admit – I repeat once again – that truth is an abstract value and what is proper to philosophy is a search for values other than in the abstract sense.[16]

AB: Does science need philosophy?

GC: I would respond that science needs philosophy and that it has no need whatsoever of philosophy if by philosophy we understand the specific production of philosophers. No science can pass philosophy by and the proof of this is that now it is science itself that elaborates its own philosophy. The sciences create a philosophy that is necessary to them, that is to say, the critique of their foundations.

Mathematics itself resolved the antinomies of set theory. And it was physics itself that sets itself to the task of responding to the question, poorly posed in a philosophical sense, of indeterminacy.

What I just said does not mean that since science does not need "philosophy" that philosophy would be lacking in meaning and does not correspond to a need.

I can still make my response even clearer: why does science need philosophy?

If it is for its own development, it does not need [philosophy]. It resolves problems by itself and poses a critique of its foundations by itself.

Hence, what is required by science that could only be satisfied by philosophy?

AB: But the question might signify something else: can science respond by itself to all the questions that it provokes in human practices? Does it respond to the questions of a philosophical order provoked [by science] in human consciousness?

GC: Let's say that the question had two meanings: the first can be borrowed from philosophers who are also scientists. Science is today para-philosophical and the problem of the logic of guardianship, critique, and canon no longer has meaning. Science undertakes its own critique.

The second meaning is that of regarding science not as an autonomous discipline but as a mode of activity having [certain] results (the exposition of a certain vision of certain sectors of phenomena) as a form of human spirit. This question is different from the first one and poses [different] philosophical questions. No science can resolve its own terrain and this non-scientific question [arises] as a capacity of the human mind. "Why does mathematics exist?" is a question that is not in mathematics and to which mathematics cannot respond.

AB: Does the level of scientific knowledge held by the students of a philosophy class allow for the useful reflections on the sciences? That is to say, under what conditions can we teach the philosophy of science or epistemology to students in the final year of secondary education?

GC: This reflection is indispensable. It is possible only if we can appropriately narrow the scope [of reflection]. Although difficult, it would not be productive unless it had some strict limits.

We should naturally presuppose that what is in the scientific curriculum and the philosophy class of the secondary school is common knowledge, in mathematics, in physics, in chemistry, in biology, and in cosmology.

Under these conditions students of philosophy can be brought to reflect productively on the commencements, and I insist on this term "commencements" of modern science. By this I mean that they can understand the meaning, the difficulty, and the progress of the cosmological revolution (Copernicus, Kepler, Galileo); that they can understand the commencement of modern mathematics with Descartes and Pascal; that in biology they can understand the meaning of the commencement of anatomy with Vesale; physiology with Harvey; natural history with Buffon and Linnaeus. I even think that they can go all the way to understand the signification of Newtonian astronomical mechanics and the chemistry of Lavoisier.

I mentioned "meaning." By this I do not refer to content or method, or even mathematical techniques. But I think it is not productive to have students reflect on science after 1800. In particular I think that a professor of philosophy should not embarrass himself in a philosophy class by speaking of modern mathematics as if he knew more than these students who began studying the elements of modern mathematics much earlier.

I add that none of this makes any sense except for in the current state of the balance between philosophy classes and the scientific disciplines. In my thinking, the actual curriculum demands only the absolute minimum for this sort of reflection to be possible. It is clear that if scientific teaching was reduced, mutilated in philosophy classes, we would have to give up any attempt to have students reflect on science productively from the point of view of philosophy. This would basically reduce philosophy to literature. To give you an image of this, it would be like cutting off one the arms of all philosophy teachers in France.

AB: You say that the level of scientific knowledge of the philosophy class would allow for the understanding of the meaning of certain commencements of science and you cited the Copernican revolution. But would the meaning of a commencement of this nature be totally undone if the conceptions of the world that preceded this revolution were not themselves understood? Should we then also propose the teaching, for example, of the Ptolemaic astronomical system?

GC: You are perfectly right. It is clearly not possible to speak of a Copernican revolution of the world if we did not know what this Copernican vision replaced. As such it is not excluded but rather recommended to very briefly present the mathematical representation of the optical appearances offered by the movement of planets relative to the stars through which Ptolemy had composed his system. It is not difficult for a student to understand the difference between a cinematic reference and a space of perception or a fixed point in visual perception.

Notes

1 The term "*épistémologie*" had been first used in 1908 by Emile Meyerson in his *Identité and réalité* (*Identity and Reality*). In the preface of this French edition of this book Meyerson, against the approach of Comte, asserted that his book belonged "by reason of its method, to the domain of the philosophy of science or *epistemology*, to use a word sufficiently appropriate and now becoming current." [emphasis original] Emile Meyerson, *Identity and Reality*, reprint, trans. by Kate Lowenberg (London: Routledge, 2002), 5.

2 The positions expressed here by Canguilhem are similar to the ones formulated by Gaston Bachelard since his 1934 *The New Scientific Spirit*. Cf. Gaston Bachelard, *The New Scientific Spirit*, trans. by Arthur Goldhammer (Boston: Beacon Press, 1986).

3 This dissymmetry between the formal and experimental science is due to Alexandre Koyré's important influence. The position that he advanced concerning the "scientific revolution" of the sixteenth century privileged the formal rather than the experimental side of the emergence of modern science. Cf. Alexandre Koyré, *From the Closed World to the Infinite Universe* (New York: Harper and Brothers, 1958). Gaston Bachelard held similar views in *The New Scientific Spirit*.

4   Nicolas Bourbaki was the allonym for a secret society of
    mathematicians that aimed to write a comprehensive "textbook" of
    the current state of mathematics in the 1930s up to the mid-1980s.
    This "Bourbaki group" was started by former students of the *Ecole
    Normale Supérieure* before the Second World War and would
    eventually become a major force in the mathematical world after the
    war. It was comprised of the greatest French mathematicians of this
    wartime generation but also generations to come and eventually,
    through the connections made through the members' wartime exiles
    in England and North America, also included mathematicians from
    these other countries. The dynamic founder of Bourbaki was André
    Weil, brother of the philosopher Simone Weil, who befriended Claude
    Lévi-Strauss in their common time of exile in the United States during
    the war, leading to the mathematical appendix of Lévi-Strauss' *The
    Elementary Structures of Kinship*.

5   Canguilhem's line of argumentation here is the one of Gaston
    Bachelard's who, opposing Meyerson's and Bergson's "continuist"
    theory of knowledge, counterposed science – characterized by the
    construction of an abstract problematic and phenomeno-technics – to
    common sense, which, occupied by images, is a potential source of
    epistemological obstacles.

6   Since the mid-1930s, Canguilhem dedicated a lot of attention to
    the history of technology and to the cognitive, historical, and moral
    aspect of technology.

7   Jean Léopold Nicolas Frédéric Cuvier (1769–1832) was a French
    naturalist and zoologist known for his researches in comparative
    anatomy and paleontology.

8   Canguilhem is referring to Book IV, Chapter 11 of Leibniz's *New
    Essays on Human Understanding* entitled "The classification of the
    sciences". Cf. G. W. Leibniz, *New Essays on Human Understanding*,
    ed. and trans. by Peter Remnant and Jonathan Bennett (Cambridge:
    Cambridge University Press, 1996).

9   Christian von Wolff (1679–1754) could perhaps be caricatured as the
    bridge between Leibniz and Kant in the passage from early modern
    thought to the Enlightenment proper. Canguilhem is here referring
    here to his central work *Philosophia Rationalis Sive Logica Methodo
    Scientifica Pertractata Et Ad Usum Scientiarum Atque Vitae Aptata.
    Praemittitur Discursus Praeliminaris De Philosophia In Genere* of
    1728. Cf. Christian von Wolff, *Preliminary Discourse on Philosophy
    in General*, trans. and ed. by Richard J. Blackwell (Indianapolis:
    Bobbs-Merrill Company, 1963), § 8, 71, S. 33.

10 The original transcript refers to the nineteenth rather than the

eighteenth century. Given all the texts and figures here, it is more likely that Canguilhem is referring to the end of the eighteenth century.

11 Paul Tannery (1843–1904) was a French mathematician and historian of mathematics. He was the older brother of mathematician Jules Tannery. Though Tannery's career was in the tobacco industry, he devoted his spare time to the study of mathematics and its history. He edited the definitive eleven-volume collection of Descartes' works (*Œuvres*, Paris: Le Cerf, 1897–1911), a series of three volumes of Fermat's works (*Œuvres*, Paris: Gauthier-Villars, 1891–96), and he published two studies on ancient Greek science. Paul Tannery, *Pour l'histoire de la science hellène: de Thalès à Empédocle* (Paris: F. Alcan, 1887); *La Géométrie grecque* (Paris: Gauthier-Villars, 1887).

12 Pierre Maurice Marie Duhem (1861–1916) was a French physicist, mathematician, and philosopher of science, known for his writings on the indeterminacy of experimental criteria and on scientific development. Duhem also made major contributions to the science of his day, particularly in the fields of hydrodynamics, elasticity, and thermodynamics. Cf. Pierre Duhem, *The aim and structure of physical theory* (Princeton: Princeton University Press, 1991); *Medieval cosmology: theories of infinity, place, time, void, and the plurality of worlds* (Chicago: University of Chicago Press, 1985); *To save the phenomena: an essay on the idea of physical theory from Plato to Galileo*, trans. by Edmund Dolan and Chanina Maschler (Chicago: University of Chicago Press, 1985); *Commentary on the principles of thermodynamics* trans. by Paul Needham (Dordrecht, New York: Springer. 2011); *Thermodynamics and chemistry. A non-mathematical treatise for chemists and students of chemistry*, trans. by Georges K. Burgess (New York: London: J. Wiley, 1903).

13 René François Dugas (1897–1957) was a French engineer who worked his entire life for the French national railways (SNCF). In his spare time he lectured at Paris' *Ecole polytechnique* and *Ecole des mines*. He his mostly known as an historian of science, especially for his works on mechanics. René François Dugas, *La méthode dans la mécanique des quanta* (Paris: Éditions Hermann, 1935); *Histoire de la mécanique* (Paris: Dunod, 1950); *La mécanique du XVII siècle* (Paris: Éditions du Griffon, 1954).

14 An echo of this idea can be found in Louis Althusser's position, inspired by Gaston Bachelard, according to which "philosophy does not have an object in the sense that a science has an object" (thesis 4 of the first lesson of his course on *Philosophy and the Spontaneous Philosophy of the Scientists*). Louis Althusser, *Philosophy and*

the Spontaneous Philosophy of the Scientists, trans. by James H. Kavanagh (London, New York: Verso, 1990), 71. This Bachelardian influence was also already present in Georges Canguilhem's 1943 "Introduction" to *The Normal and the Pathological*, where he claims that "philosophy is a reflection for which all unknown material is good, and we would gladly say, for which all good material must be unknown." Georges Canguilhem, *The Normal and the Pathological*, trans. by Carolyn R. Fawcett in collaboration with Robert S. Cohen (New York: Zone Books, 1991), 33.

15 The definition of philosophy as a totalizing discipline is present in Canguilhem's thought since his writings of the 30s. See for example the definition, borrowed from Réné Le Senne's *Le devoir*, of the philosopher as a "professor of unity" [*professeur d'unité*] in Canguilhem's 1938 "Activité technique et creation." Georges Canguilhem, *Ecrits pilosophiques et politiques 1926–1939* (Paris: Vrin, 2012).

16 The idea that philosophy deals with other values than "truth value" is a constant in Canguilhem's thought since the 1920s. Cf. Georges Canguilhem, *Ecrits philosophiques et politiques*.

CHAPTER THREE

Philosophy and sociology

Raymond Aron and Alain Badiou

First broadcast: 6 February 1965

Alain Badiou: Starting abruptly, do you see a difference between sociology and the social sciences?[1]

Raymond Aron: Sociology in its current form as well as historically should not be confounded with the whole of the social sciences.
  In the past, social science was an effort to study social reality objectively, but we don't call that sociology today and today we can respond to your question in a sociological way. In most of the universities of the world, there is a particular discipline called sociology and there are people who are called sociologists whom we should not confound with economists and anthropologists, or with linguists and ethnologists, and hence sociology presents a specificity in terms of its object and its method or both.

AB: For example, if we turn toward its object for the moment, what might the specificity of sociology be in this regard?

RA: I would say that sociology discovered its object from the moment that it understood social relations as the object of study

FIGURE 3.1 *(from left to right)* Foucault, Ricœur, Dreyfus. © Centre national de documentation pédagogique

and reflection and in its differentiation with political relation, or command-obedience, or with the political relation of collectivity, or even with economic relations. The result of this is that what is specific to social relations is at the same time particular and global. It is in this particular sense that there are other sectors of society that are studied with other concepts but the proper object of sociology is social relation as such. You find it in every sector of society and you find the aim to grasp society in a global way. This is one of the origins of sociology, not the only one, but the aim that one finds, say, in August Comte or in Karl Marx; the aim to grasp a totality is clearly essential to the intention of sociology.

AB: These necessary scientific [grounds] in sum resulted in the dissociation or what Aristotle grouped together in the *Politics* for example.

RA: Yes Aristotle's *Politics* brought forth a sketch of economics and it was at the same time sociological and political. Aristotle's *Politics* studied different sorts of cities and their different regimes were put into relation with one another in a way that we might call, in Marxian terms, the socio-economic infrastructure. You know as well as I do that Aristotle explained these different regimes, these *politéïa*, in large measure through the relation between the poor and the rich, through the place of the middle class. It is thus a sociology but a non-differentiated sociology and this differentiation clearly has two origins: a philosophical origin and a technical or practical origin.

The philosophical origin is that society should not be confounded with the state. This phenomenon began in the nineteenth century with a great rise in consciousness from St Simonian and Marxist [perspectives]. On the other hand, a century later the discipline of sociology became a particular discipline with its own proper object or, in other words, its own proper perspective. This is such that sociology takes its place as one of the social sciences but a social science with a particular character that is dedicated to interrogate its object, to interrogate its finality and, so to speak, to interrogate its own philosophy. It is a particular science but it might perhaps be the most philosophical of the social sciences. Maybe I say this because I come from a philosophical background and I have not really stopped being a philosopher.

AB: Do you think we can speak of fundamental concepts in sociology?

RA: Incontestably, most of the sociologists today, at least in the West and up to a certain point also in socialist countries, employ a conceptual system or a collection of concepts and these concepts define what we can call the sociological perspective or sociology's unfolding of the social lived reality. These concepts have their origin, first, on the one hand, in the concepts of anthropology, those of Lipton for example, the concept of the status, role and, on the other hand, what is found in Max Weber's conceptualization of the types of action later reworked by Talcott Parsons. And most sociologists use these concepts such as status, roles, attitudes, objectivity, particular, and universal, and I think that this conceptual ensemble ends up defining a type of abstract human being that I call the "*homo sociologicus*" or simply "sociological man." This is something that can be compared with the "economic man" of the nineteenth century. The economic man of the nineteenth century was the abstract schema of a subject that wanted to maximize something, its pleasure, its profit, its money. And, well, the sociological man of the twentieth century is someone in a social situation, who plays a certain number of roles and makes claims on others and on the collective and who obtains satisfaction or is denied in these claims; it is the human being defined by a plurality of roles. It is something that shows us, it seems to me, the link between sociology and social science, it is almost a sociology of the knowledge of sociology and at the same time it is true that the human being of modern societies is typically one differentiated through a large number of institutions that play different roles. It is precisely this comprehension of social differentiation that is, it seems to me, the justification of sociological conceptualization.

AB: Does the concept of ideology appear to you capable still of rendering us its services?

RA: It does render us service but in good as well as bad ways! It renders service because it incontestably poses important questions. It is dangerous because the term is equivocal.[2]

One of my colleagues who has a taste for distinctions has found 13 meanings for the word "ideology." I will save you this great number of these meanings. We can simply say that I see at least three principal ones.

First of all, regardless of which political party or individual, if one tries to synthesize one's attitude with regard to reality or one's vision of reality, we turn these abstract ideas into something that we would call "ideology." This is to say, we get a stark presentation capable of convincing someone else of one's representation of the political world or objectives. In this sense, any political party possesses a certain degree of ideology, even the most conservative ones or the least ideological ones.

There is a second meaning, the meaning that arises when we can speak of a Marxist ideology or, with a bit more difficulty, of a fascist ideology. I call this the systematic formation of what any political party possesses, that is to say, a group of ideas. And the systematization, the representation of the historical past and the future of a group provides an ideological system, something that is at the same time much stronger and much more rigorous but also more false in the sense of ideology in the weak sense that I spoke about a moment ago.

And then there is a third sense that interests me the most. This is what we find in Marx. This is ideology as false representation or a justificatory representation of the world. Starting from this point, you have a problem that is at the same time sociological and philosophical. That is, what is it to be someone in relation to the idea created by oneself? What is it to be a class or a society with respect to the idea that this class or this society created of itself? And there you have a sociological problem but a problem that is philosophically charged because it always seems difficult to me to rigorously define the pure being either of a person or a society. Maybe if you adhere to psychoanalysis you would tell me that psychoanalysis is the only means to say what is the authentic being of a person, or perhaps the being of a person is also an ideological construction on the part of the psychoanalyst or by the patient as you might have it.

AB: But the sociological man that you spoke of a moment ago is, like the man of the psychoanalyst, also something constructed.

RA: Yes, incontestably, and you cannot take up and explain social reality without transfiguring it through the use of concepts, since all science is an objectification of reality. Even if the aim of sociology is, in final analysis, to understand how a human being can live in their society, this what I believe, there is a phase of the objectification of the lived [*vécu*] that is its properly scientific phase. So, the justification of sociological objectification through concepts proper to sociology is double. On the one hand we observe the roles played by human social beings; this is not something we make up. On the other hand, we set a group of techniques to work – surveys, questionnaires, inquiries, projective tests – through which we come to objectively grasp how individuals fulfill their role and also how they think through their role. So this is an objectification but it is scientific because it is not artificial or gratuitous and is justified at the same time through the techniques employed and by the nature of the social being that we aim to understand.

AB: If I understand correctly, I return a bit to what was said before, it is in the difficulty of making a scientific or rigorous distinction between the actual being of a class or group and the discourse held by this class or group that you see, I suppose, the faulty use of the word "ideology."

RA: What I think is this: the sociologist is not at all obliged to make a radical philosophical choice between how an individual lives and the idea that she has of himself. For the belief that we have of a certain reality or that how we live is also part of reality. The way that we are conscious of our existence is the not the same manner in which others see us, but each of these perspectives or each of these consciousnesses is a part of a global reality. The danger is the dogmatism that says: "you think falsely!" or "I understand [you] correctly!" So it is here that ideology serves as a system, if you like, of a reciprocal unmasking. We could even invoke Nietzsche here. Nietzsche, in a certain way, is at the origin of what I call the ideological usage of unmasking others. In Marx also, outside the complexity of his system, one finds that each person might unmask the other. The danger is that we might arrive at a radical skepticism, a reciprocal denunciation of every position and we thus exit science and enter into polemics. The difficulty, you know as well as I do, is that when you say "this is how people live and this is how they believe they live," you are at the edge of an unmasking. Here you suggest more or less that they justify themselves by an ideology that is only partially true or by arguments that are half-refuted. Hence there is a thin line between what I would call the scientific usage of the notion of "ideology," the effort for understanding the difference between lived experience and their consciousness of this experience, and the political-polemic usage where each one denounces the false consciousness of the other. Here each one has clearly only partial reasons against the other. Except there are also facts, there are also realities, roles that we play, the distribution of wealth, the distribution of privilege, the existing hierarchy, and it is precisely because there are facts that we could objectively grasp the systematic usage of the polemic sense of "ideology" that seems to me so dangerous.

AB: I would like to ask your opinion as a sociologist on the popular concept of "structure."

RA: Yes, this is probably the one question of yours that I would respond to the least willingly, because the concept of "structure" is so terribly popular. And on the other hand it poses a series of problems. By enormous simplification, we could say that the actual use of the term "structure" such as we find in what we call the structural anthropology of Mr Lévi-Strauss has its origins in linguistics.[3] In linguistics the word "structure" has a defined meaning: each language is phonetically defined by the choice of a certain number of sounds and there are systematic relations between these different sounds that a language uses and there is a system of substitution between these different systems. Going to the other extreme, if you consider what psychologists take as form, you find a collection and you might try to define it, to determine the law of the composition of parts that constitutes a whole. In the first case, you have a sort of abstract combination, in the second case you are in a concrete structure of something considered as a whole. There was an anthropologist who used the term "structure," Radcliffe-Brown, in a concrete sense and there is an anthropologist that uses the term "structure" in an abstract and combinatory way, Lévi-Strauss. So if we generalize, we could say that what sociology tries to do is simultaneously analytic and synthetic. It is analytic in the sense that it tries to grasp all the elements one by one, and synthetic in the sense that it tries to recompose the whole that constitutes a political regime or an economic system or a global society because no social whole is [simply] a juxtaposition of elements. All social wholes bring with them a law of composition. But the laws of composition concerning an economic system are other than the laws of linguistic composition or kinship relation. And in the case of an economic system, you have quantifiable calculations: you have fundamental and simple concepts, investment, consumption, etc. So you come more simply to a concrete structure. I leave to one side the vulgar and political uses of the word "structure" or what happens when we nationalize an enterprise; we say that this is a structural reform but not in sociological terms.

AB: We have made a tour of a certain number of concepts. If we have to spell them out now, today, a discourse of sociological method, the rules of sociological method, what finally remains of the work of the pioneers, of Durkheim, for example?[4]

RA: Yes, personally, I think that the book of Durkheim that is the most outmoded is *The Rules of the Sociological Method*.[5] If you take *Suicide*,[6] for example, it is a great book for its time, a pioneering book because of its use of statistics. It was certainly a primitive use of statistics with even a few mistakes in passing from statistical correlation to the determination of types. I would say that a good part of empirical sociology in its concrete and modern sense with a much more refined use of statistics, with mathematical methods that are infinitely more developed, with facts established by surveys that are much more credible, a big part of empirical sociology, can be situated in the line traced by Durkheim.

In turn, I would say that *The Rules of the Sociological Method* is a very philosophical book. The distinction of the normal and the pathological poses a great number of questions that were not concluded or resolved by Durkheim.[7] Even the notion of considering social facts as things is an equivocal notion. Here we could mean that we have to admit them in advance such as to qualify phenomena through the validity of a pre-given rule. By this we could also mean we treat human and social reality as inanimate things and thus be in error since there is in all of social experience, in all of the lived experience of individuals and groups, what Sartre called a projection, and in what a sociologist always aims to understand, lived existences even if before arriving at this goal of understanding what is lived. We must pass through objectification: we pass through questionnaires, we pass through surveys, and we pass through statistical treatment. So personally, I do not think that *The Rules of the Sociological Method* is the best book for an introduction of sociological method.

Personally if I would make some suggestions about books, I would suggest *Suicide*. For those who read languages other than French, I would also suggest a few studies in Max Weber's *Wissenschaftslehre,*[8] essays on the theory of science which will soon be translated into French, and I would suggest a book like *On Social Research and its Language* that was published by Lazarsfeld[9] in the United States where the scientific treatment of sociological data is laid out and analyzed in detail. This does not at all mean that there is nothing to be retained in the work of Durkheim. For example the concept of anomie is still used by all of American sociology and all modern sociology; *The Elementary Forms of Religious Life* is a great book. We could say that this is the most philosophical and the least sociological book but it is the most methodological one. This is not actually so surprising since when sociologists write a methodology they [tend] to write about the methodology of their early work. That is to say that, at the end of the day, Durkheim would end up close to John Stuart Mill. Something like this ultimately turns out to be the case but this is not the last word on scientific method or authentic sociological method!

AB: You seem to consider the philosophical character of Durkheim's project as a reproach. Is this to say that sociology has nothing to gain from philosophy?

RA: Oh no! This is not at all what I mean. When he wrote *The*

Rules of the Sociological Method, in saying that, in the end, we will transform social studies into a scientific study, it is better not to imply that the rules of the method formulates a philosophy.

There are many different sorts of relations. The first relation is that which takes place between any scientific discipline and the philosophical reflection that occurs on these techniques and the methods of a discipline. In this classical way, just as we try to have students understand methods in physics or in mathematics, it is also good to have them understand methods in social sciences. In saying this, we approach only the most elementary relation. But there is another and much more important relation. That is, what sociology treats is the existence of human beings in society. So there are at least two philosophical problems that are posed here. First, how can we observe what is subjective? How can we grasp from the exterior what is a lived experience without ignoring this dimension of the lived or the dimension of projection? And secondly, to objectively study the manner in which human beings live in society brings us to problems that philosophers habitually ask. That is, how do they live? How should they live? Yet sociologists will not tell them how they should live but they can at least provide a confrontation between the manner in which they live and, through the values that they hold, how they should live. There is then a sort of implicit philosophical critique within sociology that takes place in the confrontation of a social experience of a regime, with the idea that this regime makes of itself and with the objects that it poses itself. Because of this, there is thus a sort of philosophical contribution that sociology makes to philosophy and there is at the same time a philosophical problematic inside sociology. Would this be a half-response to your question?

AB: I would be fully persuaded that you have given a half-response if you say now what the second half is.

RA: Right, this is what I had in mind. All the philosophers of the Western tradition are, in one way or another, moralists and all or almost all attached their reflections on human existence and morality to a certain explicit or implicit representation of society. And there is, it seems to me, a danger in how a moralist loses track of the social reality of her times or with the transformation of this social reality especially in times of rapid upheaval like today.[10] I do not want to say at all that ultimate moral values or the ultimate moral reflection depends on the structure of society, I don't know. At least this is the philosophical question on which I cannot come to a decision. But I think that we might renew certain classical themes of moral philosophy by placing this theme in relation to the proper problems of social order today. For example, we often discuss the common good. What does this common good mean in a society divided by classes? Or we have often spoken on the kingdom of ends, what does this kingdom of ends mean in a society rationalized and organized by large corporations like today? Sartre tells us that human relation is not authentic except on the condition that the principle of reciprocity is respected. But what does this reciprocity mean concretely between the contractor and the worker, between the executive of a big corporation and the thousands of employees in this corporation? So it seems to me that we could have students reflect at the same time concretely and in a profoundly philosophical manner by placing them in front of the social reality in which we live. It is in this sense that I think that a basic comprehension of the society in which we live is a necessary element for enriching philosophical reflection, for there is always a danger that the teaching of philosophy which is too closely tied to tradition would be impoverished and encrusted in these terms. That is, it conserves only the tradition but forgets that this tradition was alive and that it changes from epoch to epoch as a function of problems that were posed to human beings.

AB: And so precisely, and I come here to considerations that may be more limited, more practical and pedagogical. If, in the last instance, moral analysis, moral reflection, and philosophy should be nourished by a certain understanding of the concrete, the real, what is the role according to you that we should give to the teaching of sociology for example in the final year of secondary education in philosophy?

RA: First I would like our philosophy teachers to have the same contact with what we call sociology today and what we called sociology in the last thirty or forty years. That is to say that it is not so often that such a gap exists between the actual state of a living science and the idea that philosophy has of it. But philosophy cannot always be on top of what is going on in all the scientific disciplines. That's the first aspect.

The second point is that I think, without asking philosophy teachers to be specialists of all the social sciences, there is at present a sort of a third culture, a third domain between what we call the exact sciences and the pure humanities which is the set of social sciences that nonetheless possesses a philosophical project that is not exactly the same as the exact sciences. Because the object in question is the human being and this is precisely the domain of social sciences. Those who teach philosophy should understand this specificity. What are the requirements for this? I think that we could require of them, say, a basic understanding of a few essential disciplines, for example, political economy, an idea of the concrete methods employed by sociologists. It is not difficult to render understandable how we study the life of workers in a corporation, how we study social classes, how we pose the problem of the relations, of contexts, between different social groups, how we study phenomena objectively, how we can simultaneously determine the limits of an objective study with scientific results and their universal and certain validity. In other words, I think that we should understand these sciences in their proper limits for nourishing philosophical reflections without at the same time paralyzing them with the decree: "This is how things are and this is how things ought to be." This is precisely the sense in which we understand what is scientific in these social disciplines. We can use them philosophically to show the philosophical problematic within them and that the philosophical problematic is renewed by it rather naturally without being reduced to objective study. For in the final analysis, the analysis of the manner in which human beings live will never supplant the questioning, or ultimate question, of what philosophy asks itself and addresses to humanity. Social sciences are but an element of this interrogation, but I think that it is an element which has its costs and its value. And precisely in our time, since we live, I think, in a great moment of historical revolution, the type of society in which we live is of the sort that is in many regards original.

So this is very general and very simple and I think that,

without pretension, and from my own experience, that what I am telling you is what I always wanted to philosophize but it seems difficult to philosophize on politics without knowing what societies are. So, like other philosophers, one more or less philosophizes on human experience, one philosophizes on politics. How could one do so and how should one do so without knowing what social science can provide today?

AB: But this summary introduction of the living social sciences in secondary education, since this is what we are concerned with the most directly, should it be decided by specialists or should it remain as it is at present, decided by the framework of philosophical curriculum?

RA: I hope that it remains, without dogmatism, in the framework of teaching philosophy. That is to say that what I hope is that there are departments of social sciences where specialists from different social sciences deepen each others' understanding; where economists philosophize and philosophers learn political economy. While waiting for people like this to come around, I think the chosen few are still the philosophy teachers for I think that they are the ones who are capable of approaching these two aims that are essential for me. The first is to determine what is scientific in the discipline and then to mark its limits, that is to say, to find the philosophical question at the origin and at the end.

Notes

1 To understand this dialogue one should keep in mind the Althusserian critique of the "so called social sciences." Cf. Louis Althusser, *Lenin and Philosophy*, trans. by Ben Brewster (New York: New Left Books, 1971), 8. What is also significant is the creation of the first undergraduate degree (*licence*) in sociology in France in 1957. We also point to the attempt, made by Pierre Bourdieu (1930–2002) and by Jean-Claude Passeron (1930), two of Aron's students, to give new rigor to sociology as a science. Cf. Pierre Bourdieu, Jean-Claude Chamboredon and Jean-Claude Passeron, *Le métier de sociologue: Préalables épistémologiques* (Paris: Mouton de Gruyter, 1968).

2 In 1955 Raymond Aron published his *L'Opium des intellectuels* in which he used the word "ideology" to denounce certain interpretations of Marxism, especially those that had pretensions to establish historical materialism as a science. As such, what is in the background of the following discussion concerns the concept of "ideology" such as provoked by the debate surrounding Aron's book. Cf. Raymond Aron, *The Opium of the Intellectuals*, *trans.* by Terence Kilmartin (New Brunswick: Transaction Publishers, 2001).

3 This is an allusion to Claude Lévi-Strauss' *The Elementary Structures Kinship* and to the explosive debates provoked by his 1961 *The Savage Mind*. See Claude Lévi-Strauss, *The Elementary Structures of Kinship*, trans. by J. H. Bell and J. R. Sturmer (Boston: Beacon Press, 1969). See also Claude Lévi-Strauss, *The Savage Mind*, trans. by George Weidenfeld and Nicolson Ltd. (Chicago: University of Chicago Press, 1968).

4 Emile Durkheim is considered to be the founder of sociology as a science.

5 Emile Durkheim, The *Rules of the Sociological Method*, trans. by W. D. Halls (New York: The Free Press, 1982).

6 Emile Durkheim, Sucide. A Sociological Study, trans. by John A. Spaulding (New York: The Free Press, 1997).

7 Aron seems here to be referring to the implicit use, made by Durkheim, of Auguste Comte's distinction of the normal and the pathological as states differing in quantity that Georges Canguilhem (a good friend of Aron) will criticize in his *magnum opus*, *The Normal and the Pathological*.

8 Max Weber, *Gesammelte Aufsätze zur Wissenschaftslehre* (Stuttgart: UTB GmbH, 1988).

9 Paul Felix Lazarsfeld (1901–76) was an American sociologist considered by some to be the founder of modern empirical sociology for his research in statistical survey analysis, panel methods, latent structure analysis, and contextual analysis. See Paul Felix Lazarsfeld, *On Social Research and its Language*, ed. by Raymond Boudon (Chicago: University of Chicago Press, 1993).

10 The aim of the work of both Emile Durkheim and Lucien Lévy-Bruhl was one of grounding the study of society on a science, sociology, which would be capable of separating itself from moral philosophy.

CHAPTER FOUR

Philosophy and psychology[1]

Michel Foucault and Alain Badiou

First broadcast: 27 February 1965

Alain Badiou: What is psychology?

Michel Foucault: In general, when someone asks this question, especially to a psychologist, he actually asks two very different questions. First he asks, "What does psychology do?" But I don't think that this is the most important question. What is the question really asking? I have the impression that when we ask this question, "What is psychology?" we are automatically asking this other more fundamental question: "Is psychology a science?" What I am saying now is a banality but I think it is important all the same. It is important because it is publicly notorious that the scientific status of psychology is not, first of all, well established, and secondly that it is not at all clear.[2] Nonetheless, I worry that when we ask the question, "Is psychology a science?" we are probably not even asking the most fundamental question, something that would permit us to lay the ground for other questions, or at least what is essential to the other questions. I would like if we could interrogate psychology not so much from the form of objectivity that it

FIGURE 4.1 *(from left to right)* Foucault, Ricœur, Dreyfus. © Centre national de documentation pédagogique

could achieve, the form of scientificity that it is capable of, but rather to interrogate psychology like we would interrogate any other cultural form.

AB: What do you understand by "cultural form"?

MF: Well, by "cultural form"[3] I understand, if you like, the manner in which a given culture such as an organized or institutionalized knowledge frees up a language that is proper to it and eventually reaches a form that one could call "scientific" or "para-scientific." So I would like for us to interrogate psychology from this root: how is psychology a form of knowledge in Western society, a knowledge that can or cannot be scientific.

AB: From this point of view, what would be your response?

MF: Well I think that psychology belongs to a certain cultural form that is constituted in the Western world perhaps during the current of the nineteenth century. This cultural form, appearing at this particular moment, is not completely dated to the nineteenth century. It is clear that the cultural form of psychology was installed or was inscribed in turn through the history of many other cultural forms. Here, for example, I think of the confession during the Christian centuries, I also think of literature or theater. Also, we can think of [other] institutions, during the Middle Ages, or even still of the sixteenth century, courtly love, salons, etc. Ultimately, we can see that it is a sort of questioning that human beings have brought about. It is this questioning that has taken up, during a given moment, the cultural form that we call psychology.

AB: You did not mention philosophy. Is philosophy not a cultural form or, even better, is there not any relation between psychology as a cultural form and philosophy?

MF: You are actually asking me quite different questions. You are asking me if philosophy is or is not a cultural form and you are asking me whether philosophy and psychology as cultural forms have a relation. Finally, you are asking me what kind of relation could take place between two cultural forms.

For the first question, I think that we can respond by saying that philosophy is probably the most characteristic and the most general cultural form in the Western world. Since the beginning of Greek thought until Heidegger, until now, philosophy has been the means through which Western culture has perpetually continued to reflect on itself. In this sense, philosophy is not a cultural form but is the most general cultural form of our culture.

Now, for the question, "Are there relations between the cultural form that is philosophy and the cultural form that is psychology?" To this question, how could we respond? We can respond in two ways. We can say that psychology is actually something that takes up, in a positive and scientific way, a series of questions that haunted and animated philosophy across the previous centuries. And in this answer psychology, in treating behavior and comportment, actually demystifies, on the one hand, and on the other, renders positive notions like the soul, for example, or thought, etc. In this sense, psychology appears purely and simply the taking up of what had been up to this moment something that was alienated and obscured to itself under the form of philosophy in a scientific manner. And in this way psychology appears as the cultural form through which the West has actually questioned itself. This would be the fundamental relation of the human being to itself in a culture such as ours.

Now, there is another possible answer and it is this possible answer that I prefer. It consists in saying that in being the most universal cultural form, something happened in philosophy, the means by which the West has reflected on itself, at a certain moment in time in this cultural form and the reflection that it permits. Something fundamental happened at the beginning of the nineteenth century or maybe already at the end of the eighteenth century. This event was the appearance of what we might call reflection in the anthropological style. That is to say, what appeared at this moment, for the first time, is an inquiry that Kant formulated in his *Logic*, "What is man?"[4]

AB: But all the same, before Kant, there were treatises entitled "*A Treatise of Human Nature*," there were reflections on the human being.[5]

MF: Yes, but I think that reflection on human beings in the seventeenth and eighteenth centuries, all of these treatises on human nature, all of these treatises are in reality nothing but the deployment of a reflection of the second order with respect to philosophical reflection. That is to say, the philosophical problem, at least during the Christian epoch, was a reflection on the infinite. The human being does not enter into question except in relation with this philosophy of infinity. This means that we ask ourselves under what conditions and how it could be that finite beings can have, on the one hand, true knowledge, that is to say, knowledge of the infinite and nonetheless could be perpetually tied to their finitude by things like error, dreams, imagination, etc. In this way, the question "What is man?" was not, I think, the fundamental question of philosophy.

AB: And so, with Kant, there was an overturning of perspective …

MF: ... with Kant there is an overturning of perspective. That is to say that for the first time philosophy inquires directly on finitude. It is from finitude that philosophical inquiry will begin. It is also characteristic that, some time before, the thinking of the infinite had migrated toward mathematics.

AB: Even so the *Critique of Pure Reason* is not anthropology.

MF: Yes, but I would respond to you through Kant's *Logic*. You know, when Kant asked the three questions, "What can I know?", 'What should I do?', 'What can I hope?', he brought all three questions toward a fourth question, "*Was ist der Mensch?*", the question "What is man?" and in this we say that it is at the same time a question of anthropology and the most general question of philosophy. And in this way, I think that Kant is really either the founder or at least the discoverer, of a new field of philosophy that is anthropology, a philosophical field that came about, I believe, in the nineteenth century through the intermediary of the dialectic, through Hegel, through Marx, in order to cover the domain that was traditionally one that belonged to philosophy.

AB: Will you allow me to summarize what you have said in a few sentences that would be unfaithful to what you have said certainly ...?

MF: Certainly not ... [chuckles]

AB: You have distinguished two perspectives. In the first, philosophy in sum opens up the domain of psychology but the human sciences take it up in an effective and positive way. In the second perspective which we have underlined as your preference, anthropology is entirely taken up as an end point in philosophy as the cultural form through which the West has come to think of itself or attempts to achieve self-reflection. So, if you like, I would like to ask my question again relative to the essence of psychology at both of these levels. First, if we admit that philosophy had totally and implicitly prescribed its domain to the human sciences in general, where human sciences would be the storehouse of old philosophical questions, in this perspective, by admitting that you could provisionally mime it, what gives the specificity of psychology in the context of these other projects that we designate commonly as the "human sciences"?

MF: Well, I think that what characterizes psychology and that which makes it the most important of all the human sciences and that which renders its status, was Freud's discovery of the unconscious, that is to say psychology itself, within the self, working in the end of the nineteenth century as a transformation that was absolutely surprising. This is what I believe opened up the most problematic questions in psychology. We can basically say that psychology since the end of the eighteenth century and until the end of the nineteenth century had essentially given itself the explicit task of analyzing consciousness, the analysis of ideas under the form of ideology, the analysis of thought, the analysis of feeling etc. At the end of the nineteenth century there was suddenly, pivoting around its object, a psychology that was no longer that of a science of the conscious psyche but a science of something that had just been discovered, the science of the unconscious. Well from the moment where psychology was discovered as a science of the unconscious, it was not simply or did not simply act in such a way as to incorporate this new domain, a domain that was unknown until that moment. It did much more. It entirely restructured the domain of all the human sciences. In effect, through the discovery of the unconscious, psychology discovered that the body is itself part of the unconscious and that the collectivity that we belong to, the social group, the culture in which we live is part of our unconscious. It reveals that our parents, our father, our mother, are nothing other that the figures of our unconscious, etc. As such all the sciences neighboring psychology like physiology, like sociology, were then remodeled and remade with psychology in mind in the meditation of this discovery of the unconscious. The result is that psychology thus became, at the level of foundations, the most elusive one. It probably became that which carried, in itself, the full destiny of the human sciences.

AB: Let us now move to another perspective. What place would you assign to the Freudian discovery of the unconscious in anthropology understood as a philosophical moment in Western thought?

MF: Well in this, a certain number of events took place, you see, I continue to speak of events. I am fierce partisan of an evental [*événementielle*] view of history at least in philosophy since, after all, until now, we have never taken up the history of thought except for in abstract terms and general structure, through the ideal and the atemporal. And so we should maybe attempt a purely evental history of philosophy and not that of philosophers. If we undertake this evental view of the history of philosophy I think that we would need to observe a series of facts or events basic to the very existence of philosophy as it occurred in the nineteenth century. This unconscious that psychology discovered as a new object and at the same time as an absolutely universal method for all the human sciences, we see that this unconscious was in fact already reflected upon by philosophy itself since Schopenhauer. That is, this unconscious was a philosophical object since Schopenhauer and remained so until Nietzsche's revival [of the question]. At the same time, the anthropological question in philosophy was what Kant had assigned to philosophy as its most general domain. Thanks to the reflection on unconsciousness, we realized, if you like, to speak very generally, that man does not exist.[6] This is really what Nietzsche discovered when, in affirming the death of God, he showed that this death of God is not simply the end of the Christian religion, this was also not the end of all religions, but this was the end of man, of man in its reality and in its humanistic values, the end of what was constituted since the Renaissance and since Protestantism, or perhaps even much earlier since Socrates. And so we arrive at this very curious chiasm in the fundamental events of Western thought in the nineteenth century. This was the appearance of anthropology as the destiny of Western philosophy at the start of the nineteenth century, rendered by a philosophy as the unconscious as, at the same time, the foundation and the disappearance of this anthropology. And on the other side, the human sciences and psychology once again took up this unconscious at the end of the nineteenth century, in founding the human sciences in the form that aimed at [this unconsciousness], that believed in it and perhaps attempted to render it positive. But from the moment when the human sciences were founded in their positivity we find that man had philosophically disappeared. And if there exists today precisely this relation or non-relation between philosophy and psychology, it is perhaps directly due to this phenomenon. On the one hand philosophy had imposed the anthropological theme on Western culture and then at the moment when psychology took up this anthropological theme and gave it, thanks to the unconscious, an absolutely new and perhaps positive voice, in this case philosophy discovers that man itself does not exist. This renders the positivity of psychology as founded on nothing but this aberration, this void, this lacuna that is the existence of man.

AB: You have said that the great recentering of psychology and much of the human science in general was done at the end of nineteenth century around the theme of the discovery of the unconscious. The word "discovered" was taken in general in a scientific or positivist context. What do you mean exactly by the discovery of the unconscious?

MF: Well I think that we should take the word more or less in its strict sense. Freud literally discovered the unconscious as a thing. There has been for twenty-some years a current trend that says that regardless of the other aims of psychoanalysis, we encounter a perpetual thing-oriented [*chosiste*] postulate in Freud. Ultimately, since Politzer[7] until and including Merleau-Ponty, this thing-oriented thinking, the positivism of Freud was critiqued as an after-effect of nineteenth-century thought and we tried, on the contrary, to reintroduce something troublesome like the unconscious, and to reintroduce it in a network of significations that are more subtle, more detailed, in the network of significations as such. In such a way, the unconscious could take a place in terms of a transcendental subjectivity or perhaps an empirical or historical one. Regardless, the unconscious had ceased to be this terrible and rocky thing that Freud had discovered that is somehow underneath the human psyche. But ultimately, we should not forget at the same time that Freud had effectively discovered the unconscious like one discovers something or rather, if you like, as we discover a text. We know very well – and here the interpretations of Dr Lacan on Freud are uncontestable – we know that the Freudian unconscious has the structure of language. But this does not mean that the unconscious is some kind of empty or virtual language, that is to say that it is not a system that allows us to speak. It is something that is basically written, texts that are actually within the existence of the human being or in the psyche of human beings if you like. In any case, it is literally discovered when we practice this rather mysterious operation that is psychoanalysis. We discover a written text, that is to say that we first discover that there are sedimented signs; secondly, that these signs mean something, that they are not absurd signs; and thirdly that we ultimately discover what they mean.

AB: The understanding of the unconscious as a text and then the operation through which we decipher the signification of this text, are these two methodological moments of psychoanalysis?

MF: It seems that in the practice of psychoanalysis, the discovery that there is a text and the discovery of what the text means are not really one and the same thing.

AB: Does this mean that, using the language of linguistics, the discovery of a psychical text is at the same time the message and the code of this message?

MF: We have a collection of markings, if you like, for which we do not yet know if they are letters or representations of words; even more, when we find out or we assert that they really concern sedimented words, we do not know their meaning and we don't know the relationship between them and their meanings. We thus need for the analytic operation to all at once perform a triple act. That is, first to isolate the signifier, secondly to establish the law that governs the relations of the signifier to the signified and finally to discover what it means, to discover the final text that there is to interpret.

AB: Yes but here I see a difficulty. If the message that the unconscious represents is its own code, psychology in the form of psychoanalysis will reveal the inability to constitute itself as a science of general structures. We would face in all these cases simply individual texts, particular codes limited to themselves and this demands of us to reconceive the whole enterprise each time.

MF: Well this is why there is no general psychoanalysis at the base of it all and this is why there is no collective psychoanalysis. We cannot speak of the psychoanalysis of a culture, for example, or a psychoanalysis of a society except metaphorically. That is to say, we find ourselves in the domain of science through error and abuse of language. There is only individual psychoanalysis and only in this absolutely foundational act of meaning that is there an analytic relation to medicine, between the psychoanalysis and its patient. However this does not mean that each of these discoveries, these rigorously individual discoveries, cannot allow us to establish certain isomorphisms or certain general structures of language that we will find in another individual. But the fact that the message rests in itself its own proper code is a fundamental law of psychoanalysis and this means that there is no psychoanalysis except within this individual operation that is the psychoanalytic cure.

AB: I would like now to return with some obstinacy to the question of what psychology is. Perhaps here I am forcing you to talk about what I suspect you do not wish to speak on. You define psychology as a science or knowledge of the unconscious but ultimately, what status would you accord to these other practices, to these existing practices: animal psychology, psychological testing, psychophysiology, factor analysis ...?

MF: In brief, all this is what we call, in contradistinction to psychoanalysis, theoretical psychology or laboratory psychology. Well, it seems to me that this psychology is less theoretical that we could imagine. I mean here that the sort of distinction between Freudian theory and practice is certainly not the one that we have believed it to be for a number of years. Freudian practice and Freudian theory were certainly not the one and same thing. On the contrary, so-called theoretical psychology seems to me to be terribly practical. I mean that the relations of production have changed between the nineteenth and the twentieth century, and the human being appears to be something that is not simply a producer but now rather as a consumer. And it seems to me that a part of this emergence of consumption as essential economic fact and also in the stakes that it has in its relation to production has opened up an interior space where a certain number of practices have become possible. The psychology of aptitudes, if you like, and the psychology of needs appear to me to all reside very well in these new economic practices. I think that all psychology from the moment of its departure from psychoanalysis is basically a psychology of the economic sort.

AB: We have often, at least during a certain period, distinguished or counter-posed experimental or positivistic psychology and anthropological psychology with the distinction between explication and comprehension. Is this [still] meaningful to you?

MF: I think that this is meaningful and is very profound but I am not sure that the notion of comprehension is absolutely the best one. It seems to me, if you like, that what took place is basically the following. Since the eighteenth century until the end of the nineteenth, all the interpretive or exegetic disciplines had in some way or another remained in the shadows or had retreated to the shadows of a methodology of knowledge that aimed much earlier at a definition of the laws or principles of explication that were more or less positivist. And so through Nietzsche and also through the reappearance of exegesis and interpretation of religious texts in the nineteenth century, and clearly also through the discovery of psychoanalysis and the interpretation of signs, we find that interpretive techniques reappeared in Western culture. These interpretive techniques were founded in Alexandria even before Christianity and never ceased to underlie Western culture until the sixteenth century, until the Renaissance or perhaps until Cartesianism. And it is the reappearance of these interpretive techniques that Dilthey[8] described with a word that is perhaps not the best one, that of "comprehending." I would prefer if we used the difference between explication and *interpretation*. This appears to me a better characterization of this movement through which the ancient Alexandrian exegesis reappeared to us through Freud and contemporary psychoanalysts.

AB: Well I will finish with a pedagogical question. If you would have taught in one of our classes in the final year of secondary school what we call "psychology," how would you do it?

MF: Well, I should tell you that I would be rather embarrassed because I have the feeling that I would at least have a double role. On the one hand, I would need to teach psychology and on the other hand I would teach philosophy. It seems to me that the only means to resolve this problem is not to ignore the split but, on the contrary, to insist on it and to underline it even more. And what I would like to do is to create a course of disguised psychology, disguised like the philosophy of Descartes. But here I would disguise myself as a psychologist. I would attempt to change my face as much as I can, to change my voice, to change my gestures, to change all the trappings of my *habitus*. During the hour dedicated to psychology, I would teach laboratory psychology, I would teach psychological testing, I would teach the maze, I would teach the rat. Of course, I would also have to speak about psychoanalysis and this would be, if you like, the second variation of this first persona. I would try to speak with the strictest prudence but with the greatest precision of what psychoanalysis is, which is so close to the foundation of the human sciences and nonetheless so far from laboratory psychology, probably because it is not tied to the same structure of praxis. And then during the following hour, I would be a philosopher. That is to say I would take off my disguise, I would try to use my own voice, and it is in this moment that I would, in every way that I can, as myself, speak of what philosophy is.

Notes

1 This version of the interview is the one transcribed for and published in the *Cahiers philosophiques*. It strongly differs from the one published in Foucault's *Dits et écrits*. Cf. Michel Foucault, *Dits et écrits Vol.1* (Paris: Gallimard, 1994), 438–48. This present version is a translation of the more direct transcription before being submitted to Foucault's revision. Cf. *Cahiers philosophiques* 55 (June 1993).

2 Michel Foucault refers here to the debates between philosophers and psychologists that erupted at the moment of the institutionalization of

"scientific" psychology at the end of the nineteenth century, but this can really be dated back to the beginning of the nineteenth century and to the opposition between, on the one hand, the proponents of a positivist and medical approach to the human psyche, such as Victor Broussais and Auguste Comte after him, and the proponents of a "spiritualist" psychology such as Maine de Biran and Victor Cousin after him. But overall Foucault refers to the famous 1958 talk of his mentor, Georges Canguilhem, "What is psychology?" Cf. Georges Canguilhem, "Qu'est-ce que la psychologie," *Revue de métaphysique et de morale*, 1 (1958); republished in *Les cahiers pour l'analyse*, 2 (February 1966). In this text, Canguilhem argues against Daniel Lagache and both criticized the instability of the epistemological status of the discipline and its political implications. Cf. Daniel Lagache, *L'Unité de la psychologie : psychologie expérimentale et psychologie clinique* (Paris: PUF, 1949).

3 Michel Foucault first defines psychology as a "cultural fact" in his 1961 *Madness and Civilization*. Cf. Michel Foucault, *Madness and Civilization: A History of Insanity in the Age of Reason*, trans. by Richard Howard (London: Routledge, 1996), 199. Foucault then consecrates an entire chapter to this in his 1962 *Maladie Mentale et Psychologie*, a modified version of his 1953 *Maladie Mentale et Personnalité*, entitled "Psychopathology as a fact of civilization." Cf. Michel Foucault, *Mental Illness and Psychology*, trans. by Alan Sheridan (Los Angeles: University of California Press, 2008).

4 The following developments implicitly refer to the final part of *The Order of Things* and especially to the eighth section of the Chapter 9 chapter entitled "The Anthropological Sleep." Cf. Michel Foucault, *The Order of Things* (New York: Vintage Books, 1994), 341.

5 Badiou might be referring to David Hume's early text, *A Treatise of Human Nature*.

6 This refers back to Foucault's conclusion in *The Order of Things*.

7 Georges Politzer (1905–40) was a psychologist, a philosopher, and a Marxist militant executed by the Nazis. In his famous *Critique of the Foundations of Psychology: The Psychology of Psychoanalysis* he tried to reform the contemporary trends of psychology (behaviorism, *Gestalt* psychology, and psychoanalysis) from what he considered its "realist" language and operations. His interpretation of psychoanalysis, based on the notions such as "signification" and "drama" and the critique of the notion of the unconscious as a reservoir, influenced a whole generation of intellectuals: Sartre, Merleau-Ponty and especially the young Lacan. Foucault's first book, *Maladie mentale et personnalité* was also implicitly influenced by

Politzer who was the main inspiration for Marxist psychologists during the 1940s and 1950s. Cf. Georges Politzer, *Critique of the Foundations of Psychology: The Psychology of Psychoanalysis*, trans. by Maurice Apprey (Pittsburgh: Duquesne University Press, 1994). Cf. Michel Foucault, *Maladie mentale et personnalité* (Paris: PUF, 1954).

8 Wilhelm Dilthey (1833–1911) was a German historian, psychologist, sociologist, and philosopher. Inspired by Friedrich Schleiermacher, he is considered as one of the initiators of modern hermeneutic philosophy. Cf. Wilhem Dilthey, *Selected Works*, ed. by Rudolf A. Makkreel and Frithjof Rodi (Princeton: Princeton University Press, 1991–6).

CHAPTER FIVE

Philosophy and language

Paul Ricœur and Alain Badiou

First broadcast: 13 March 1965

Alain Badiou: Does the philosopher have any particular reason to be interested in language?

Paul Ricœur: There are two sorts of reasons: traditional reasons and new reasons. The traditional reasons are due to the fact that philosophy has always been a struggle for clarity, for clarification and for coherence. And in this aim its work is a linguistic work of a particular and privileged form. It is in reflection and in philosophical speculation that all the problems of signs and meanings from other disciplines are contemplated. The history of philosophy shows us that philosophy has always been a struggle against the defects of language, against poorly posed questions and traps of language. Hence philosophy is in a struggle with its own language. But, on the other hand, the problems we are facing today come from particular disciplines, from the science of language. It is in this sense that the contemporary philosopher as well as the philosophy teacher has the particular task to reflect on the philosophical problems in the methods and results of the squarely scientific discipline of language, that is, linguistics.

FIGURE 5.1 *(from left to right)* Canguilhem, Foucault, Dreyfus, Ricœur, Hyppolite. © Centre national de documentation pédagogique

AB: Between the positioning of the problem of language such as we find, for example, in Plato's *Cratylus* and this considerable transformation of scope that you are now speaking of, do you see continuity or rather a mutation?

PR: We can begin with mutation. This stems from the fact that linguistics is a science and it is an exact science and a domain that has deeply influenced, through the great advancements of phonology,[1] the whole of the human sciences. It is from phonology that linguistics was reconstituted and it is from this reconstitution that the philosophical problem of language has changed.

But it has not changed in such a way that would forbid us to say that everything is already in the *Cratylus*. The problem for philosophy is to know how to anchor our language and all the languages that vary according to different historical communities and according to different people in what Plato called *eidos*, the idea: the person on the street, the professional, the scientists, and finally the philosopher. But even in Socrates' own attempt to respond to the Sophists, he confronted a fundamental difficulty that is still our own today. That is, on the one hand, language is not, in its very nature, adequate to its object and nonetheless, on the other hand, languages are not so chaotic or so arbitrary that it cannot serve as a means of communication, a means to distinguish between things and create relations.

Also, we see how the protagonists of the *Cratylus* oscillated between two impossible theses. Either we hold the natural character of language as if it had the strictness of law or we hold it as arbitrary and without any rules. Plato was then searching for what we could call an unreachable origin. This is a point where language would, through a foundation, be given its role through a determination of identity.

AB: In this overcoming, in the attempt at a solution to this antinomy, which is in short the same impasse of the *Cratylus*, does the rise of linguistics help philosophy or does it, on the contrary, complicate the problem?

PR: It complicates the problem in the sense that the progress of linguistics is evident in a very limited field which is the domain of phonology or the signs of language, phonemes which are small in number. Their function is one that is essentially diacritical, a word that we already find in Plato. That is to say that it permits us to discern and to distinguish meaning.

As such, from phonology, that is to say, from the point of view where signs have a distinctive function, linguistics has really created a new situation. But the problems that are closer to the concerns of philosophy are the problem of the meaning of words and the problem of implication; these are two large domains of semantics. If we generally define semantics as a domain of meaningful unities in contradistinction from the domain of syntax, there still remain some domains that are certainly considerably renewed by contemporary research but which has not achieved the degree of rigor in phonology. This is probably because the proper problem of phonology is that of the distinctive values of unities, the distributive function of phonemes and this does not identically correspond to the domain of semantics. The meaning of a word is not simply its differential value, it is also a range of meanings and each word actually represents a field of significations with a hierarchical ordering and, as such, these pools of meanings encroach on each other. And we encounter the problem of the multiplicity of meanings, that of polysemy.

AB: Rather than the now scientific development of diacritics that constitutes the phonological heritage of the work of Saussure,[2] it is, if I understand correctly, the problem of this encroaching or equivocity of meaning that we find at the center of your reflections.[3]

PR: I think that there should be a central philosophical reflection here that consists in taking polysemy as the central phenomenon of language. This would then allow us to understand that metaphor is perhaps just as central in the constitution of our discourse as that of discrete units of language since at each moment meaning is larger than the meaning that we transmit.

This creates a considerable problem. Logic constitutes a limited domain where we can chase after polysemy. We should perhaps admit that univocal language should not be anything else than islands of language but cannot serve to reconstruct a whole language which functions on the basis of polysemy.

AB: The act of speech would be basically polysemic in principle.

PR: The act of speaking consists in controlling and regulating this polysemy. At each instant the speaking subject speaks in order to express the situation, the state of a thing or, in a general way, a series of thoughts; any use of words where the potential of meaning is larger than what one will have recourse to. Hence the possibility of speaking presupposes that I set aside an available part of the richness of meaning that is determined by the context. The maps of meaning that in general occlude each other are present for the speaking subject. And it is in the process of composition and the combination, in a process of weaving that Plato called a warp and weft, that the simplest process of predication can be understood, two meanings mutually defined. As such, the determination of meaning is made contextually and one who receives the message is also in possession of a richness of meaning that makes up part of the lexicon of culture and reconstitutes the intended sense from this abundance of meanings that one has at one's disposition.

AB: But here it seems to me that there is something a bit delicate that deserves, it seems to me, some clarification. Should we understand that when we speak meaning comes through polysemy and gains from this polysemy? Should we rather understand, on the contrary, that meaning is established against a polysemy through a struggle to constrain and through a certain way of mastering and controlling this polysemy?

PR: Yes, I would say that it is always in a struggle with or against polysemy. With, because the very possibility of signifying something presupposes what I earlier called a "potential of meaning" which is greater than the actual use that I make of available significations. On the other hand however, the work of speech that has communication as an aim presupposes an univocity, it presupposes that only one meaning is transmitted. I believe that it was Aristotle who said that "not to have one meaning is to have no meaning."[4] The central problem it seems to me is thus that this relation to univocity, and thus of meaning, with equivocity, should be that equivocity is not a disease of language but a condition of its proper function.

AB: Hence, the norm of language, its *telos*, would be, if I understand correctly, its univocity. Yet the condition of language, that is to say its natural element or milieu, is equivocity.

PR: I believe that we are here at the heart of the philosophical problem of language – that is, to understand its relation between this aim of univocity and this condition, one might even say its destiny, of the equivocity of language. Certainly, we could obtain a partial or perfect success in constructing islands of language that would be entirely ruled by univocity. This would be the domain of languages that are well defined such as in mathematics and logic.

But can we think of the totality of human language in all its functioning as being reconstructible under the model of a well-defined language? We have reasons to think that these well-made languages satisfy a certain number of constraints for resolving a certain number of problems in relation with the most advanced axiomatization of sciences. This might allow us to finally attain mastery over the technique of the world but the comprehension of human beings in its condition, its communication on the level of its available means, the level of politics, cannot be reconstructed on this model. It is against this that what I understand a well-defined and regulated polysemy as the task of speaking correctly and thinking correctly.

AB: Are there disciplines where the equivocal and the polysemic is the object?

PR: The first group of disciplines where the problem of multiple meanings is posed not only as an obstacle but also as its daily bread, as its object, is the exegetical disciplines. That is to say, these are disciplines, since exegesis is an exegesis of a text, for which the text is susceptible to a number of satisfactory readings. At its basis, it is here that we see that whatever has a meaning can also have another meaning.

But we are really in face of a problem where polysemy is

not accidental but, as we might say, essential, since the text is the carrier of a number of meanings that are not only enclosed within a text but constitutes a number of them. This is a problem that was encountered in the interpretation of biblical texts, with the Rabbis, in the first Christian generation. This was a problem that was encountered by the stoic philosophers with respect to the myths of Homer and Hesiod and in Greek tragedy. This was a problem encountered in the eighteenth century in its efforts for a rigorous philosophy. In sum, there is a meaning of meaning and when we are confronted with this problem of multiple meanings that structures a text, we encounter a question that we now call hermeneutics.[5] We might distinguish hermeneutics and exegesis in the following way. Exegesis is the interpretation of a text and hermeneutics is a reflection on the rules of reading that orders the exegesis of a determined text. If so we are obliged to construct this notion of hermeneutics in this way, in any case according to a very ancient tradition, because it is not only textual exegesis that demands this problem of us. We now have a vast palate of disciplines that we could call hermeneutic.

Dilthey[6] had already, at the start of the century, considered historical comprehension itself to already be a hermeneutic understanding in the sense that an event, a period, an institution, is susceptible to many meanings. It is in any case this unfolding of history that we find, through a recurrent taking up of events, with different meanings deployed of this same event, history as always a sort of reading of events of the past, like a text that one will never finish deciphering.

But we do now have a discipline of the first order of importance that we could consider as a hermeneutic discipline in the sense that it enters into the field of language: this is psychoanalysis.[7] If we say that a dream not only has a meaning but that this meaning is latent, and the hidden meaning is not given in means other than the apparent one and through the interpretation of this apparent meaning, then what is in question is the "public" text of the account of the dream and the text that we need to bring about through all the disciplines within psychoanalysis. This relation directly poses a question: what is then this region of meaning where meaning is the meaning of meaning, where a multiplicity of meaning is then constitutive of a domain of language?

AB: I would then like to ask two questions. The first is the following one: what relation is there between hermeneutics and the philosophy of language that you spoke of at the beginning? Should we conceive the philosophy of language as a sort of general hermeneutics? That is, psychoanalysis, biblical exegesis and the like are all particular disciplines. They do not fully belong to philosophy.

PR: In effect, the philosophical task is unavoidable since each exegetical discipline basically aims to create a univocal situation. By this I mean that the psychoanalytic interpretation will look for meaning along its own rules of interpretation. It is this form of univocity that the analyst will search for and it is the structure of psychoanalytic theory that will resolve the problem. We are not in the presence of a wild interpretation but an interpretation that attempts to be coherent along the principles provided by psychoanalytic theory.

To be more precise, I mean that all these dreams, myths, symbols, folklore, legends will appear before the court of psychoanalysis from the point of view of a driving aim which is that they are disguised and figural expressions of desire. The problem of philosophy seems to arrive at this moment. These different language games[8] that will then be laid out before us through their different rules of reading proper to each herme-neutic theory remain, if we hold to a purely linguistic map, scattered games. And what is proper to a philosophy which, for me, would be, *par excellence*, a philosophy of reflection would be to regroup these partial discourses for understanding how they would together participate in what I would call the comprehension of the self. This is to say that to understand the text is to understand oneself and I have to understand myself since there is no intuitive cogito. It is through the signs of my existence, signs in a history, signs in a culture that I will be able to decipher the meaning of my own existence as a thinking and speaking subject. And thus the task of a reflexive philosophy[9] it seems to me is to understand how the readings made at different levels and according to different rules come to insert and implant themselves in a fundamental philosophical problematic. It is thus in philosophy that we take up, in a reflexive movement, the intention of these different readings and to provide justification from the starting point of a philosophical problematic. This is why I recuse any capitulation of philosophy before linguistics. If there would no longer be a reflexive taking up of meaning, we would have nothing more than a lexical or syntactic analysis. If we cut ourselves off from the comprehension of meaning in a work of thought from the understanding of ourselves, in other words, if we separate hermeneutics from reflection, we would have nothing but language games.

AB: And so, I would then ask you the second question: in your generalization of the notion of a text, would you also apply this to the image?

PR: This poses a problem of knowing if we have the right of speaking of a pictorial language or a musical language. I highly doubt this. I think that, in this case, we use language analogically. We do not know what is signified before signs are articulated. It is in a domain of articulation that language begins to take place. This does not forbid that we retroactively push back after this has taken place, in some way, the values of signification onto pre-languages or para-languages. But it continues to remain in analogy.

After all, this is not different, for example, to the problem of animal intelligence. We know what is intelligence for a being that speaks, which has a logic and so we can push our ideas down toward a domain where we clearly know what is meant and to see what might be a sort of prefiguration of this meaning. This is what Plato called a bastard reasoning. The work of art is a work of someone who also speaks. But this reasoning allows us to apply meaning to an encounter with the signifying productions of beings who do not speak. The set of signs produced by the painter or musician who are speaking subjects, those who organize by their colors or their sounds with respect to in their signifying universe, cannot have meaning outside of their articulation in a linguistic manner.

There is then an analogy because there is an appearance in a whole domain of signs but also because those who operate these signs are also those who speak. There is then a sort of contamination of different orders of signifiers. Language is thus not simply the reference for us to reflect on but it is also the presupposition upon which those who operate in other signs. Since they manipulate linguistic signs, they also have the disposition of other non-linguistic signs.

AB: What would then become of the signification of the aim of general semantics expressed by Saussure?[10] And its theory of sign as a unity of a double: signifier and signified. Should this be limited to a domain of language properly speaking?

PR: What seems to me as specific to language is that it is articulated, in the sense that, first, it is articulated at the level of meaning. As such, the linguist Martinet[11] will speak of a first articulation, this is an articulation on a semantic level. What characterizes speech is that we operate in this first level through a second articulation that would be a sonic articulation, the phonic articulation. In sum, to speak is to maneuver two articulations at the same time. That is to say, to signify a semantic articulation through a phonic articulation.

But this signifying-signified distinction is not entirely dependent on articulation. In effect one of the latent contradictions of Saussurian linguistics has been one that its successors have aimed to resolve. That is, to bring to the surface two forms of analysis. On the one hand it concerns the sign as the carrier of a signifier that, for itself, is an acoustic image, and, on the other, that of the signifier which is still interpreted in a rather psychologistic manner, through the concept. The signifier-signified relation is thus a relation that is in sum vertical and at the interior of the sign. On the other hand, Saussure placed each of these signs in a horizontal or lateral relation, each sign is nothing except for its precise place in the articulated character of the linguistic domain, as a difference within the system.

This differential relation of each sign in a collection of signs is a phenomenon that is properly linguistic. But I think that we could say, following a Saussurian line, that the signifier-signified relation has a universal scope for semiology. This is to say that the sign constitutes a fundamental phenomenon and perhaps is in certain regards foundational to the humanity of human beings. The fact that each sign stands for something else, this referentiality points to a sort of absence of things and of the world, a global withdrawal with respect to the full presence of things, [all] this constitutes the institution of the sign. In sum, we might, in a philosophy of language, start with the possibility of sign such as it is defined by human beings, this withdrawal from the immediate and full presence of things and thus this "value standing in for something" that brings about the world of signs. As such, this entry into the world of signs results in all the semiotic registers that we were equivocating on just a moment ago without enumerating them and the linguistic sign is the absolutely privileged domain of signs or articulations. As such the diacritical value that the *Cratylus* already names is the rule of constitution.

AB: I would now like to ask you some questions of a pedagogical sort. As a philosophy teacher I have a double relation to language. I have to treat the problem language, one of the chapters of the curriculum of philosophy and on the other hand, I have to treat, as we know, the enunciations of philosophy, that of the transmission of philosophy. From this, a double question. You have spoken of a revolution in the problem of language and I would like to know first if this revolution has any consequences in the very way in which we pose the problem of language in a philosophy course. My second question concerns the language that the teacher of philosophy should employ when one aims at the transmission of philosophy or the transmission of the teaching of philosophy to students.

PR: Your first question is the most simple but finally the most embarrassing one since in a philosophy course language is at the same time the title of a part of the course and at the same time a milieu, the element in which we produce what follows. It seems to me that this makes language, the philosophical problem of language, implicitly present in each section of psychology. I would even say this relates to perception since what could we really know of human perception? What can I understand of human perception that is not articulated by a speaking being? What can I know that is not stated?

Bachelard has taught us that the image is much less the result of a mental spectacle as the product of a rebirth of a speaking being.[12] The problem of logic is really the problem of *logos*, and a *logos* that is *legein*.[13] As such speech, discourse, and logic are problems that adhere one to another. There is hence a sort of diffused treatment of the problem of language at all levels of philosophical pedagogy. And it seems to me that the task of a section on language would be to take up the philosophical problems of language from the starting point of a conscious language. Starting with Saussure, we could treat the sign as a signifier-signifed, the problem of language as a system of differences, the relation of language-speech, language as what is in a linguistic community, speech as the act of a speaking subject. At the interior of this Saussurian world of linguistics, we can consider a sketch of how it contributes to what is properly scientific in linguistics from the basis of phonology. Here we take up the problem of semantics in the sense that it at the same time attains the status of a scientific linguistics through constant revision but at the same time never resolves or even leaves indefinite these problems for the reasons that I pointed out earlier, the problems of polysemy that does not fit into the mould of a distinctive function, the guiding star of phonology.

And as such, we could allow classical problems of philosophy to reappear, the problems that have stayed with us since the Sophists, since Socrates and the *Cratylus*, in a sort of turning back from the Saussurian and the linguistic revolution. And in sum, this consists in placing the totality of the project, the philosophical project, into what is, in the present, localized in linguistics.

AB: This brings me to my second question. For a teacher of philosophy, there is a problem of the use of language in philosophy itself. This language is at the same time presented as a technical language that plays its role in determining rigor and it is also a language saturated with history. For this reason, it is often equivocal and even obscure and mysterious in particular for our students. What do you think of this difficulty? More generally, what is the status of philosophical language?

PR: There is in reality two versions of your question. On the one side, philosophical language is distinct from scientific language in that it has a history and is part of a tradition. As such in any given moment in language, in the system, and in the philosophical lexicon that we have at our disposal, there emerge all the meanings that are present in history. This situation is unavoidable because we cannot have a philosophy that is without history and we also cannot have a philosophy without it being at each instant taken up by its own history. As such, philosophical language is under the reign of a polysemy that holds sway through a silent presence of its entire history and its present. But on the other hand, philosophical language represents a rupture with respect to ordinary language and so to initiate young people to philosophy is to bring them into an enclosure where language is already constituted, or, as I would say, Plato existed and Descartes and Kant and so on. Hence no one ever begins philosophy. To philosophize is always to continue and it is to insert oneself into a moment of philosophical discourse. We then find ourselves in something of an additional difficulty, a problem that we have been brushing up against from the beginning of this interview and the problem with which we will conclude. That is the question through which we began, what we called a moment ago this "struggle with or against polysemy."

I think that one of the weapons, one of the resources that we have is that, in order to comprehend philosophical texts, we should always take words within their context. We cannot first decide on a new and univocal meaning of the world "intuition" for example. We understand it alongside all of the different branches of meaning that starts from Plato and goes all the way to Bergson, but we can actually articulate these meanings at each moment through their larger contexts. This is why the comprehension of philosophical vocabulary is inseparable from the comprehension of the philosophical text and in this regard, there is no shortcut to this initiation, that is to say, this leap into an enclosure, this entry into a regime of thought and of language that is philosophy. We need to enter into exchanges with great philosophers since they are the ones who have created philosophical language: we do not begin a philosophical discourse, we continue it.

[The transcription of this interview is followed by an "*Explication de termes*" – a lexicon of three terms: phonology, semantics, and hermeneutics. They were not part of the interview but are reproduced here from the transcription]

Phonology:

Phonology is the branch of linguistics that takes up the form of articulation proper to the phonic expression of each language, with the exclusion of the articulation of the meaning-units (see the comments on "semantics" below): "This phonic expression is articulated in turn in distinctive and successive unities. Phonemes are determined in number for each language, for which their nature and different mutual relations also differ from one language to another."[14]

Semantics:

In the strict sense of the word, semantics is this "branch of linguistics that treats the articulation of unities of meaning or words."[15] Morphology is the study of their forms and the lexicology of the collection constituted by semantics and morphology. The distinction between morphology and semantics can be secondarily extended to the lexicology of syntax. That is, to the relation of discourse: it thus designates the function corresponding to diverse grammatical forms. In order to distinguish between these two usages, we might adopt the following rule: "Whenever the term semantic is employed in a linguistic context without a qualifying adjective, it concerns lexical semantics; when concerns the study of relational meaning, it should explicitly mean that we speak of syntactic semantics."[16]

Hermeneutics:

This word first designates the set of rules that preside over the exegesis of a text. By extension, it designates all applied interpretations of a set of signs susceptible of receiving multiple meanings. This art of interpretation concerns semantics in its distinctive trait; the multiple meanings that interpretation brings about is here actually articulated in such a way that the meaning considered as the most fundamental is at the same time shown and hidden by the most immediately accessible one.

Notes

1 For these technical terms, please refer to the notes at the end of this interview.

2 Ferdinand de Saussure (1857–1913) is generally known for his posthumously published *Course in General Linguistics* whose ideas laid the foundation for many significant developments in linguistics in the twentieth century. Though his thought was already known by French linguists at the beginning of the century, the structural paradigm implicit in his synchronic linguistics become widespread in France during the late 1950s and the 1960s when it began being massively employed in the human sciences by Claude Lévi-Strauss, Jacques Lacan, Roland Barthes, Algirdas Julien Greimas. Ricœur began following the developments in linguistics around 1962, after the major polemics and discussions provoked by Lévi-Strauss' *The Savage Mind*. Ricœur participated in a reading group on the anthropologist's book organized by the editorial board of the *Esprit* journal that ended in a dialogue with the author. Cf. Ferdinand de Saussure, *Course in General Linguistics*, ed. by Charles Bally and Albert Sechehaye, trans. by Wade Baskins (New York: Columbia University Press, 2011). Cf. Paul Ricœur, "Réponses à quelques questions," in *Esprit,* 31, 11 (1963): 628–53.

3 Ricœur treated for the first time the problem of equivocity and univocity of meaning in 1965, in the first part of *Freud and Philosophy: An Essay on Interpretation*. Cf. Paul Ricœur, *Freud and Philosophy: An Essay on Interpretation*, trans. by Denis Savage (New Haven: Yale University Press, 1970).

4 Aristotle, *Metaphysics*, Book IV, Chapter 4, 1006b7.

5 Following Martin Heidegger's turn, Ricœur was interested in hermeneutics, at least since his 1960 *The Symbolism of Evil.* Hermeneutical thinkers argued that language is the primary condition for all experience and that linguistic forms (symbols, metaphors, texts) disclose dimensions of human beings in the world. Paul Ricœur, *The Symbolism of Evil*, trans. by Emerson Buchanan (New York: Harper and Row, 1967).

6 Wilhelm Dilthey (1833–1911) was a German historian, psychologist, sociologist, and philosopher. Inspired by Friedrich Schleiermacher, he is considered as one of the initiators of modern hermeneutic philosophy. Cf. Wilhem Dilthey, *Selected Works*, 5 vols, ed. by Rudolf A. Makkreel and Frithjof Rodi (Princeton: Princeton University Press, 1991–6).

7 Ricœur showed an interest in psychoanalysis since his 1950 PhD
dissertation, *Freedom and Nature*, and in 1965 published his first
book explicitly consecrated on the theme, *Freud and Philosophy: An
Essay on Interpretation*. In France the crucial importance of language
in psychoanalysis had been underlined by Georges Politzer and
then by Jacques Lacan. Cf. Paul Ricœur, *Freedom and Nature: The
Voluntary and the Involuntary*, trans. by Erazim Kohak. (Evanston:
Northwestern University Press, 1966).

8 Here Ricœur is probably referring to the concept of language games,
Sprachspiel, that Ludwig Wittgenstein developed in the *Philosophical
Investigations*.

9 Other than that of the tradition of phenomenology and hermeneutics
Ricœur inscribed his work in the legacy of reflexive philosophy. Jean
Nabert (1881–1960), to whom Ricœur devoted a series of writings
such as his 1957 review of Nabert's *Essai sur le mal*, his 1962 essay
"L'acte et le signe selon Jean Nabert" and his 1962 and 1966 prefaces
to Nabert's *Éléments pour une éthique* and to *Le désir de Dieu*. In
these texts, Ricœur considered Pierre Maine de Biran (1766–1824)
as the founder of a tradition of reflexive philosophy that would be
continued by Jules Lachelier (1832–1918), Jules Lagneau (1851–94)
and Léon Brunschvicg (1869–1944). In *From Text to Action: Essays
in Hermeneutics*, Ricœur defines reflexive philosophy as "a mode of
thought stemming from the Cartesian *cogito* and handed down by way
of Kant and French post-Kantian philosophy." According to Ricœur,
this type of philosophy "considers the most radical philosophical
problems to be those that concern the possibility of *self-understanding*
as the subject of the operations of knowing, willing, evaluating, and
so on." Reflection is considered to be "that act of turning back upon
itself by which a subject grasps, in a moment of intellectual clarity and
moral responsibility, the unifying principle of the operations among
which it is dispersed and forgets itself as subject." Cf. Paul Ricœur,
Lectures II (Paris: Seuil, 1999). Cf. Paul Ricœur, "L'acte et le signe
selon Jean Nabert," *Les études philosophiques*, 17, 3 (1962): 339–49.
Paul Ricœur, *From Text to Action: Essays in Hermeneutics II*, trans.
by Kathleen Blamey and John B. Thompson (Evanston: Northwestern
University Press, 1991), 12.

10 Here Badiou seems to confuse semantics with semiology. In the
3rd chapter of De Saussure's *Cours*, "The object of linguistics," De
Saussure writes: "Linguistics is only a part of the general science of
semiology, the laws discovered my semiology will be applicable to
linguistics, and the latter will circumscribe a well-defined area within
the mass of anthropological facts." De Saussure, *Cours*, 16.

11 André Martinet (1908–99) was a French linguist, influential for his work on structural linguistics. He is known for pioneering a functionalist approach to syntax proposed in his *A Functional View of Language* and in *La linguistique synchronique*. His *Elements of General Linguistics* (1960) has been translated into seventeen languages and has influenced a generation of students both in France and abroad. Cf. André Martinet, *A Functional View of Language* (Oxford: Clarendon, 1962); *La linguistique synchronique* (Paris: PUF, 1965).

12 Ricœur quoted Bachelard's studies on imagination in his *Freud and Philosophy: An Essay on Interpretation*. Cf. Paul Ricœur, *Freud and Philosophy: An Essay on Interpretation*, 15–16. We will find an echo of these remarks in his 1975 *The Rule of Metaphor: The Creation of Meaning in Language*, "Bachelard has taught us that the image is not a residue of impression, but an aura surrounding speech." Paul Ricœur, *The Creation of Meaning in Language*, trans. by Robert Czerny, Kathleen McLaughlin, John Costello (London: Routledge 2003), 254.

13 *Logos* comes from the Greek verb *legein* which has two meanings: "to speak, to say," or "to pick, to gather."

14 André Martinet, *Eléments de la linguistique générale* (Paris: Armand Colin, 1960), 25.

15 Pierre Guiraud, *La sémantique* (Paris: PUF, 1959), 9.

16 Stephen Ullmann, *The Principles of Semantics* (Oxford: Blackwell Publishing, 1951), 33.

CHAPTER SIX

Philosophy and truth

Georges Canguilhem, Dina Dreyfus, Michel Foucault, Jean Hyppolite, Paul Ricœur, and Alain Badiou

First broadcast: 27 March 1965

[Excerpt from "Philosophy and its history"]

Jean Hyppolite: No, I would not employ the word "error." [...] [I]
t seems to me too general to speak of an error at the interior of
a philosophical system. It seems to me, if you like, difficult, for
example, to take a whole class of philosophers and say: "There
we go! Descartes was mistaken about doubt." Or, "Descartes
was mistaken about this or that ..." I do not think that a
philosopher is refuted by another philosopher, even if they take
themselves to be refuting one another, I do not think that the
refutation of a philosopher by another philosopher is something
that makes much sense. [End of excerpt]

[Excerpt from "Philosophy and science"][1]

FIGURE 6.1 *(from left to right)* Canguilhem, Foucault, Ricœur, Hyppolite. © Centre national de documentation pédagogique

Alain Badiou: Do you think that there is philosophical truth? Are you going to scandalize us here?

Georges Canguilhem: Oh! I don't think I would scandalize you personally. But I would say: there is no philosophical truth. Philosophy is not the sort of speculation whose value can be measured by true or false …

AB: So what is philosophy?

GC: Because we cannot say that philosophy is true, this does not mean that it is a pure language game or purely gratuitous. The value of philosophy is something different from truth value whereas truth value is something that is reserved specifically for scientific knowledge. [End of excerpt]

[Scene I]

Jean Hyppolite: I am in total agreement with what you said on truth: "There isn't ..." Maybe in the past we could have spoken of a truth in philosophy and a truth in science to the degree that the sciences existed. It is irreversible today to the degree that there are sciences that are now established and there are no longer plural truths. And there is no contradiction between what you have said, that there are only scientific truths, and what I said that there is no error, alas, perhaps, in philosophy.

Georges Canguilhem: Yes, there is no contradiction but yet it is not exactly the same thing to say "there is no error in philosophy" and to say that "there is no philosophical truth." First of all that there is no error in philosophy flatters all the philosophers! But it is very clear that where is no error there is no truth either properly speaking.

JH: Nor wandering, in such a way that ...

GC: Absolutely agree. In this way I am also totally persuaded that there is no contradiction [between us] and in any case it seems to me that when I said that there is no philosophical truth, I didn't mean by this that, in the first place, a philosopher never has the task of knowing whether she speaks is truthful and, secondly, that a philosopher is, because of this, estranged from the investigation of nature, or sense or essence, or as you say, of truth.

JH: I think that we should differentiate between truth and the problem of the essence of truth.[2] This is not the same sort of thing as scientific truth. The essence of truth concerns a different register. This is similar to saying that "the essence of technology is not technology." We should say more exactly that the essence of truth is a problematic where we might, as it were, err, but this is an authentic problem with respect to the specialized truths of current sciences. Scientific truths today are essentially cultural, they are no longer cosmological. Einstein was perhaps the last [of his kind]. There could not be a Newton today. We can no longer write a history of the sky, a cosmic problem, it is no longer possible. Ultimately, no physics either. This point was one that Bachelard already saw clearly. [Scientific truth] is something cultural, and the word cosmic is no longer employed by Bachelard except in what concerns poetry, never in what concerns truth.

GC: ... in the imaginary and never in what concerns the rational.

JH: A sense of totality only remains in philosophy and we could not at all evacuate this from our vision.

GC: No, this is the very definition of philosophy.

JH: The more sciences become cultural and less cosmic, less totalizing, the more it will need a philosophy to unite human beings. Philosophy will be that much more indispensable while science gets closer to truth, rigorous and technical truth, the truth of a special domain. The more it will need a return to this essence of philosophy.

GC: Absolutely agree.

[Excerpt from "Philosophy and language"]

Paul Ricœur: [P]hilosophy has always been a struggle for clarity, for clarification and for coherence. And in this aim its work is a linguistic work of a particular and privileged form. It is in reflection and in philosophical speculation that all the problems of signs and meanings from other disciplines are contemplated. The history of philosophy shows us that philosophy has always been a struggle against the defects of language, against poorly posed questions and traps of language. Hence philosophy is in a struggle with its own language. [End of excerpt]

[Scene II]

Michel Foucault: ... You said above in your emission that the ends of philosophy, well, the goal that it aims at, was the clarification of language and coherence, the establishment of a coherence. And in the course of this emission you spoke of a fundamental polysemy of language. Is there not something of a contradiction here? There is a certain opposition that recuperates a bit of this apparent opposition between Canguilhem's position and that of Hyppolite's. Hyppolite said that there could not have been error in philosophy and Canguilhem said that there is only truth in science, science on the side of coherence, and philosophy perhaps on the side of polysemy.

Paul Ricœur: Yes, I think that this contradiction should be introduced into philosophical work. On coherence I would not say that it is a requirement but a means that we are obligated to pass through, a path that is opposed to philosophy and from which poetry entirely separates us.

However this coherence could never be a formal ideal for philosophy because what comes to the surface in the field of philosophy is first all the inherited languages and these carry along with them their piled-up significations, ordinary language, the problems inherited from reflecting on science, on technology. It seems to me then that philosophy should be considered as a space of confrontation between, on the one hand, the formal task of coherence and on the other hand, the effort to get a hold on what is ultimately in question for philosophy, that is, through this multiplicity of meaning, what is.

MF: That is to say that polysemy would be either on the side of ontology or on the side of cultural contents delivered and transmitted by history and coherence would thus be on the side of the very form of discourse.

PR: When we spoke before of communication, this communication with oneself or with others is the formal map of discourse ... but I do not think that we could reduce philosophy to its proper formality. It seems that philosophy brings us to a more primitive question, which is primordial. This is the question, say, of Aristotle: What is?

[Scene III]

MF: Is it not being itself that is in question for philosophy?

Dina Dreyfus: You have already discussed this question between yourselves I suppose. For me, there are three questions that are tied together in this problem that we are treating today; the first question, the first point, is an apparent contradiction, one that I would say is very apparent. This is between Hyppolite's position, "there is no error in philosophy" and Canguilhem's proposition, "there is no philosophical truth." In any case, Hyppolite's position has been interpreted by certain people as meaning "philosophy is never wrong" ... I think that it is not what it means.

The second question is then the elucidation of your own conception, Canguilhem.

And finally, the third question which is in my view underlying the other ones is the question of the signification of the philosophical enterprise. What does it mean to philosophize? These three points are related. I don't think that we could look at one in isolation. We need to look at them altogether.

JH: We [actually] agree on this seeming contradiction because I did not sense this difficulty when I read his [Canguilhem's] text. It seemed to me perfectly complementary to what I said. There are no truths in the plural sense and only scientists working today can be faced with error and that philosophy cannot be wrong. Having said this, there are great philosophies and there are philosophies that do not exist.

GC: I am a bit surprised by the idea that I was poorly understood. I said that "there are no philosophical truths" but I did not mean that "there are no truths in a philosophy." A philosophy can be wrong if it ends up in paralogisms. I wanted simply to say that a philosophical discourse on what the sciences understand as truths cannot by itself be called true. There is no truth of truth.

JH: For example, for Kant the transcendental analytic represents a type of truth. This is no longer true for us today. It is no longer truth in the sense that there is no transcendental which has its own truth today. I think that Foucault agrees with this. We are in an anthropology that has gone beyond this. We are no longer in a transcendental.

MF: What currently constitutes the anthropological base on which we unfortunately reflect on too often is precisely a transcendental that aims to be true on a natural level ...[3]

JH: ... but which cannot be!

MF: ... which cannot be. From the moment when we try to define an essence of the human being that might be stated starting from this essence itself and might at the same time be the foundation of all possible knowledge and of all possible limit of knowledge, we will then actually have two levels in truth: truth and the truth of truth.

DD: Listen! Listen! Do we hold or do we not hold that there is a truth of the philosophical discourse as such? That is, could we say that a philosophical system is true or false?

MF: Personally, I do not hold this, unfortunately, there is a *will* ...[4]

DD: You have said, you say, Foucault, that there is a will towards truth, there is an aim towards truth. But even if we aim at truth and we do not reach it, it is nonetheless the norm of truth that is in question in this case. And this is actually what is in question: Is there a norm of truth for philosophy? I believe that Canguilhem would not agree.

GC: No. I do not hold that there is a norm of truth for philosophy. It seems to me that there is another type of value for philosophy, to use a more general term, than that of truth.[5]

PR: Yes, but isn't this because you started off by thinking the problem of truth in terms of norms and criteria? I wonder if the question of truth isn't the last question that we could ask ourselves rather than one that is pre-given. It is not that by starting from an epistemological model we could then ask the problem of truth but rather it seems to me that we should start from another question. It seems to me that the fundamental question of philosophy is what is. So if the first question is "what is?" then the first question ... the theory of knowledge is secondary with respect to the theory of being and science is itself, secondary with respect to knowledge. This is even so in what you call value, should we not call this *truth*, if we define truth as the most complete possible grasp in discourse of what is? If you allow that there is a problem of value for philosophy, the field in which you integrate scientific value and other values, this is precisely the field where a problem manifests that I earlier called truth, that is, the treatment of being by its discourse, and then you would never but have a form, I would not say a deposed one, for it is a rather privileged form, but a derivative form of truth in scientific truth.

GC: I might respond to your question in a certain way, by rejecting it. I would reject your definition of truth, the grasping of discourse and what is. Because precisely for science what is is defined progressively as something true independently of all relation to a supposed being as a term of reference.[6] It is in the sense that certain philosophies conserve a realist definition of truth. In this confrontation of discourse and being we can hold that, in drawing conclusions from what we understand today, in science, in truth, we can draw the conclusion that philosophy can, in remaining faithful to its fundamental project, define or at least to glimpse its own value, its own authenticity, without assuming for itself the concept of truth. Here it is clearly understood that [philosophy] treats truth to the degree that it is the space where the truth of science confronts other values, whether they be aesthetic or ethical values. There you go ... it might not be perhaps very clear but I never said anything other than this during my discussion with Alain Badiou.

JH: Could I simply intervene here in saying that you said that there is neither object nor nature, nor cosmos, nor universe, for science. At the present moment, the sciences, in their extremely specialized aspects, establish their truth entirely. To this degree we reserve this totality for ourselves. In this we are caught up, we are held in *this* totality: nature, cosmos, human beings.

GC: I have said nothing else.

PR: And so, this relation to totality, this is the question of truth. I clearly understand that these historical forms are contemporaneous with certain forms of science rather than with others.

Philosophical statements are also then given to aging insofar as they are correlated with a state of the sciences but the very question is to know that I am, I am in what is, and that at the same time I testify to my situation, I have projects and that it is in this context that I carry out my projects, I illuminate something through which a discourse is possible. This is the network of reality. Because if we do not call this truth, but rather call this value, the relation between different values in play in our human existence will find itself entirely cut off from this question of totality. In other words, the idea of totality is the way in which we rationally recuperate this relation between my being and being.

GC: Yes, it also occurs to me that I didn't mention something else to you, my dear Badiou. When I said that totality is not on the side of nature, cosmos, the world, that we could find it and this was precisely the *business*, the business proper to philosophy. That values should be brought to confront each other at the very interior of a totality and that precisely it cannot be presumed and that you cannot, according to me, give it the signification of being in the sense of the metaphysicians that you referred to a moment ago. Well it seems that I could … and I am not saying that I am right in this, since it would be to contradict my own axiom, it seems to me that I am charged with conceiving the proper task of the philosopher as one that is not specifically expressed in this mode of judgment in terms of the values true and false.

JH: Would you agree in saying that it is no longer possible today to have a philosophical thought that resembles that of ancient ontology, that is to say, to a pre-given theory? Hence since there is no longer theology there is then also no longer any pre-existing objective categories for science …

GC: There is no theology, there are no pre-existing objective categories for science. And so I am not surprised to see that among the auditors there might be those who are surprised … you said, my dear Badiou, that I caused a scandal. I do not believe that I could scandalize you. I am even certain that I will not scandalize you, but you are among those who were surprised by the proposition that I aimed toward. There are those for whom philosophy is ultimately a substitute for theology or those who think that they now have the means to transform philosophy into science.

JH: ... into objective categories that substitute an active revolutionary thought.

PR: These objective categories are already the degraded forms of their proper question. And it is this question that we need to uncover.

JH: Absolutely agree! Absolutely agree!

PR: Now this question is related to truth. How would you call this relation that we have with this question if it is not a relation of truth? If not you would end up with a grouping together of your values and their confrontation with each other is simply a cultural aggregation. Cultures precisely make manifest certain combinations of values and culture is the historical place of the confrontation of values. However what is [actually] in question when we say, with Descartes, the Descartes of the cogito, "I am"? Thus the question that is implied in the question "I am," this question here, is not tied to the history of a culture. It constitutes another dimension.

GC: It is perhaps another dimension but, if you will allow, you said to me: "What corresponds to the question who am I? to being, could I not call this truth?" I would answer: I cannot say that it is *truth* as a question. I might go as far as to call *truth* a response.

PR: Yes, it is the question of truth.

GC: I didn't assert anything to the contrary. The question of truth is perhaps a philosophical question. But a philosophy, to the degree that it proposes as an answer to this question, cannot be ordered according to the criterion of true and false in relation to another philosophy that gives a different answer. In other words, personally, I cannot say that Kant or the philosophy of

Kant is true or that Nietzsche's is a false philosophy. There are ridiculous philosophies, there are rigorous philosophies but I don't know of a false philosophy and as such I don't know of a true one.

PR: Yes, but we are interested in philosophy because each one constitutes an internal relation, in short, between its questions and its answers and in so doing determining the field, in short, of its own truth. It interests us because we have the conviction or the hope that through these finite works the human mind produces an encounter with the same being, without which we would be in schizophrenia. But at the same time we don't have the means to show that it is the same thing. This is why all we could say is that we hope to be in truth but we cannot assign truth to a philosophical system produced in the history of our culture.

[Scene IV]

AB: I would like to bring the question into perhaps a more elementary and at the same time more positive terrain. You have yourselves shown, in accord with the general inspiration of contemporary epistemology, that science does not discover the truth or does not reveal a reality that might precede it but that it institutes or constitutes, at times together, the problem of truth and the effective procedures through which, partially, this problem can receive a series of ordered responses. Would you accept then to say that science is not that through which human beings discovers truth, but that science is historically the cultural form that institutes in some way, on a terrain of validity, the problem of the truth. If you admit that human beings are, in short, the producer of truth historically under the form of a scientific practice then, as in all production, there is a problem of ends, or *telos* of production. And as such I would agree in saying that philosophy inquires, no doubt, not on or is not itself a production of truth but rather it inquires into ends, on the destination of this particular productive event.

GC: It seems to me that we said, during the course of our interview, I think that I said, at least what I can remember, that the question of the possibility of science is not a scientific question. The why of mathematics is not a question for the mathematician. Science constitutes truth, without finality, without the finality of the truth. Its finality is the truth, but there is no finality of truth for science! And so the interrogation of the finality of truth, that is to say for example what we can put into practice [???], this has always been a fundamental philosophical question, what we can put into practice [???], this is precisely philosophical. But it seems to me that all modern philosophy since Kant is characterized by the following: that the knowledge of truth is not sufficient to totally resolve the philosophical question.

JH: Would you allow me to assert that the sciences speak a technical language approaching that of an univocal language and constitutes in itself truth in the strict sense of the term?

GC: Yes.

JH: This language has a certain code,[7] that is to say that it is instituted from certain expressed conventions but this language which has a certain code is itself tied to natural language. We do not start from data, we begin from natural language, which is no doubt spontaneously ontological in the face of philosophy which can no longer be so today. Regardless, natural language is its own proper code while all the other languages have a code through their relation with this language. It thus remains a certain space in which all the technical problems of truth which are discovered by science, which has become more and more cultural and specialized, encounter one another, a space from where we take off and where we return. If I dare to say, and I hope that philosophy teachers would not think me unworthy, that true philosophy today is obliged to be a certain vulgarization in the best sense of the term. By this I understand that it is obliged to re-translate what will become untranslatable in the near future because even the intersections of sciences are themselves special sciences. We could not say that biochemistry or computer science, all these are specializations of intersections. In this way we have poorly understood your [Canguilhem's] thought, we believed that you wanted to establish truth in the sense of scientism, like "the future of science" or like Straus, but not at all, on the contrary, there are truths! And there is a space where the essence and existence of truth sprouts up in its completeness, from the start to the results. Thus it seems to me that with respect to your question: philosophy certainly began science and this was followed by its taking flight and one day philosophy under a certain form will end in order to give birth to another more indispensable philosophical thought ... But there is something irreversible here, we cannot remake ontology in the way that Aristotle did, we can no longer do ontology like Descartes did ...

PR: And at the same time, I can perfectly understand what is in question in the great philosophies of the past and what these philosophies were looking for. To put it in your language, the space from which they start and the space towards which they aim is no longer a space that is forbidden or closed to us. This is why the history of philosophy is not the history of science. You said that there is no error in philosophy but we might also say that there is no progress, no question is abolished or expires, while in the history of science, the history of technology, there really is something that becomes definitively lost. In relation to the sciences, I can at the same time understand, for reasons of development of the sciences, what we call questions of existence. This same question was called the question of being in Greek philosophy. This recognition of the same place of origin and the same place of destination of philosophical discourse is hence what permits us to speak of a problem of truth.

AB: Would you accept us saying that a philosophy is something that is a center of the totalization of the experience of an epoch which is extended across the ambiguity of relations that brings itself to operate within the framework of a code or a language which on the one hand imports the criteria of rigor, or even coherence, of science.[8] From this we would have at the same time a definition of a philosophical project and, I believe, know the value and the signification of this project independently from the notion of truth in the strict sense, or in the way that you have brought it to bear. We employ on the other hand a sort of norm with regard to this project, a finality from which this project takes up its meaning and its dignity. At the same time we might perhaps take into account the ambiguity and difficulties that are produced locally in the confrontation between science and philosophy to the degree that in different epochs – and this may have come to an end today – philosophy could have believed that this general totalization of the experience of an epoch in which it was engaged might be formulated in an analogically rigorous language in relation to the model or the paradigm that science provided for it.

PR: Yes, but here at the same time, we should not let these philosophies fall into the simple category of cultural products, products that might serve as points of historical concentration, but at the pain of losing what was in question in these philosophies and might also serve as turning points in the history of philosophy. If we lose the sense of continuity in philosophical questions and as such of the space in which these questions are brought about, we simply end up doing a sort of cultural history of philosophy and not a philosophical history of philosophy.

JH: There are two questions in what Badiou said that puts this relation into question. To say that philosophy is the center of the totalization of our epoch is basically to say that – and this was basically my conception[9] – it is a dialogue with all the philosophers of the past as if we could isolate this historical relation of philosophy. Like philosophy, these are things that are quite different and it follows that there was in our history when points of novelty were essential at certain moments, but this does not make the dialogue with these past philosophers disappear. It could be that before the birth of philosophy, with the pre-Socratics, there would be a certain means of posing the problem of philosophy and of being that were tied together because science was not a factor. And it could be that there was an epoch where science appeared almost self-sufficient in itself. There is an epoch of Newton who brought about certain types of philosophies and an epoch where there could not be a Newton and perhaps not even an Einstein. Here philosophy is again required to present itself in a different way without breaking our dialogue with the past. But in order to think about an epoch it is also essential to think of its novelty, do you agree?

AB: Yes, I agree, but it seems that if philosophy at the heart of its own trajectory should in sum mediate itself through its own history, this means that it finds in this history the instruments that are progressively forged and these constitute the category of totality. In other words, it seems to me that it is the category of totality as such that founds the continuity of philosophical discourse.

JH: This is what I wanted to get away from, this is a conception of philosophical problems drawn from a *philosophia perennis* in which I do not believe.[10] I believe in a dialogue of philosophers, in the mediation of philosophers, and I believe much more in philosophical thinking such that I do not hold an independent history of philosophical problems through philosophical figure. You see, this is what I am against.

PR: In this sense we cannot repeat any philosophy but we can understand the questions and I take my question as an issue of comprehending these philosophies.

JH: Exactly.

GC: It may be true that philosophy is the totalization of the experience of an epoch in the sense that this experience contains within it modes of experience such as science or technology, but science and technology (naturally, I am not talking about art) are activities that disqualify or depreciate their own past, and this is even something in their essential functioning ... The integration at a given moment in mathematics such as that of Hilbert or in physics like that of Einstein, or a form of art like, for example, the painting of Picasso, the integration of the modes of experience precisely [possible] because certain of these modes carry with themselves a progress. This integration can never operate in the same way even if the intention or the project of totalization remains identical. As such if there is no homogeneity of philosophies, that is, of these attempts at integration through the relation of their procedures and as such also of their style and their results, we cannot then confront one with another under a certain relation that might be called, more or less, true and we return again to my proposition from the other day. Philosophies are distinguished from each other not because some are truer than others but because there are philosophies, as all three of you have spontaneously said, that are great and others that are not.

DD: How do you understand this? In other words, is there a criterion for greatness or rigor?

GC: I don't think that there could be a criterion. If there were a criterion you would end up making me say what I did not want to say up to this moment. There are perhaps signs through which we could recognize a great, a minor, or mediocre philosopher, as I mentioned a moment ago. If it is true that philosophy should be popularized in a non-vulgar way, as Hyppolite said, this popularization of different codes adopted by the science in their path of constitution, through all the cultural activities of a given epoch, it seems to me that there is a fundamentally naïve side, I would even say a popular side, of philosophy that we tend too often to neglect and perhaps a great philosophy is a philosophy that left behind an adjective in popular language. Plato gave us something "platonic," the stoics delivered something "stoic," Descartes delivered something "Cartesian," Kant something "Kantian" as well as a "categorical imperative." In other words, there are philosophers who, because they totalized the experience of an epoch and succeeded in disseminating themselves outside of the philosophical but in the modes of culture which would themselves be totalized by another philosophy and have in this sense a direct impact on what we could call our common experience, in our daily lives, our quotidian experience. As such, it seems to me that this criterion, this clue, excuse me, could seem vulgar but I wonder if it is not nonetheless philosophically authentic.

DD: Even if we are mistaken when we say that something is "stoic" or "stoicism," even if one is mistaken in the vulgar acceptance of these adjectives?

GC: One does not need to understand Cleanthes and Chrysippus and nonetheless know what is stoic and what stoicism is. It is in any case an attitude which was promoted and reflected on by a philosopher.

JH: In such a way a great philosophy is a philosophy that is capable of being translated in a certain way into the common language of all. Simply put, we should also distinguish totalization which we are all in agreement on and a totalization, in order to have a point of impact which is often a partial totalization and through the point of impact something almost partial. In this way the sharp character of philosophical genius – for we find something here, something that touches genius – comes into contact with its own epoch, not through the work of their inheritors, that is to say, not in what is accumulated but rather in a deep contact with what the epoch pronounces in a stammer.

GC: Certainly.

PR: I would not want us to end on such an apparent agreement!

GC: It would be better if we do not agree.

PR: There is a point where I resist your view. It is a point, if you like, of bringing us to a sort of a social signification. It seems to me more important to ask if a great philosophy is one that presents the power of coming together which is the equivalent with a relation with reality or with being and I would say that a great philosophy is one that provides an impression of truth. This social index is a sort of sign that shows but which also hides the importance of the stakes.

GC: Oh yes! We can place the accent on "showing" or "hiding." Personally, I would rather place emphasis on the showing.

PR: Yes but I would simply say that we cannot reduce social influence to a single criteria which is also a relation of each partial segment of totality which we called earlier a space of encounters between philosophies where the question of truth or even the truth remains its own question. This presumption of truth can also found in what is readily felt in popular sentiments: that a great philosophy puts into words what is our relation with each other, something that varies in history but remains fundamentally the same.

GC: I would not say otherwise and this is why I prefer to let you say what you just did and allow myself to add that it is one of general sentiment rather than the social. I did not want to speak of a social and general criteria, it is the sign of a certain authenticity.

PR: For myself, I do not want to separate authenticity from truth.

GC: And for me, it seems that my defense is that I do not see why we employ the same word and the same concept in two different senses.

DD: But you, Alain Badiou, you are a teacher and when you define a philosophy as a center of totalization of the experience in an epoch, does this afford you some means in the teaching of philosophy? What do you teach through this title?

AB: In any case we do not teach philosophy dressed up in this definition. This would be to give a dogmatic teaching that actually proceeds from this totalization. This would be something like the course of Hegel or a course on scholastic philosophy. As such in the rigorous sense of the term, in the basic teaching of philosophy in any case, we do not philosophize. So what do we do? Well I believe that we teach students the possibility of philosophy. That is to say that through a series of detours in the examination of doctrines and texts, through the examination of concepts by walking through problems, we show them what is possible in the operation of this totalization. And I would even define the teaching of philosophy as the teaching of the possibility of philosophy or the revealing of the possibility of philosophy. If not there would be no other recourse than teach a [particular] philosophy and this is what our teaching aims to guard against.

DD: And from the point of view of teaching would it be possible to draw some conclusion on the debate that has been occupying us? I mean the question of philosophical truth or non-truth.

AB: It is a difficult question on which you do not agree and I do not believe that we should dissolve this disagreement. It seems to me that the space of your disagreement is limited to two agreements which are despite all else essential. First you all agree that science is one of the places of truth. In other words, it is fully meaningful to speak of scientific truth or scientific truths. And on the other hand you also all agree that the question of essence of truth is a properly philosophical question which does not as such fall into the field of scientific activity. Philosophy consists in asking from a point of view of totalization what a human being should be, what relation it has with being in order for the human being to be something that has truth. In short, philosophy perhaps does not interrogate the truth but on the *telos* of truth with respect to human existence. For some this definition supposes that philosophy itself brings out a sort of fundamental or foundational complicity with the norm that it aims to investigate and that it basically carries out in the light of this norm. For others, this question supposes on the contrary that philosophy, in interrogating the space of the truth, exits from this space and should invent its own forms. Whether the status of truth is one that is controllable, actualized, and precise remains the object of our disagreement; this is the horizon of our dialogue. Whether it is an aiming at the true or an opening towards the true, this is perhaps what we have asked in our questions and how we have understood our questions and have as such formulated our responses.

Notes

1　This except is taken from an edit of "Philosophy and Science" that is not included in the version in this volume. Canguilhem says something very similar but this excerpt is not reproduced here. See infra.

2　Jean Hyppolite shows his Heideggerian framework in his analysis here. See introduction to this volume, infra.

3　Foucault's anti-anthropological stance here be can found also in *Madness and Civilization* (1962) but expecially in *The Order of Things* (1966). Both Foucault and Hyppolite on this point are implicitly influenced by Heidegger's analysis in *Kant and the Problem of Metaphysics*. Cf. Martin Heidegger, *Kant and the Problem of Metaphysics*, trans. by Richard Taft (Bloomington: Indiana University Press, 1990).

4 Here Foucault, in a Nietzschean manner, appears to subordinate the question of truth to the will to truth and hence its *value*.

5 For Cangulhem positions here see "Philosophy and science" in this volume, infra.

6 Here Canguilhem's position is essentially based on Gaston Bachelard's non-Cartesian epistemology according to which knowledge is neither a process of passive observation nor of intuition but rather the active construction of abstract models. Cf. Gaston Bachelard, *Le rationalisme appliqué* (Paris: PUF, 1949).

7 Following the developments of structuralist anthropology and of genetics, at the beginning of the 1960s Hyppolite became interested in information theory which seemed to both confirm and complicate the Hegelian idea that the *concept* is immanent to reality. See for example the three essays ("La machine et la pensée," "Langage et être, Langage et pensée," and "Information et communication" gathered in the section "Langage et pensée" of his posthoumous *Figures de la pensée philosophique*. Jean Hyppolite, *Figures de la pensée philosophique* (Paris: PUF, 1991), 891–971.

8 In this passage Badiou appears to be attempting to integrate all the elements and main themes of "structuralism" in the framework of Jean-Paul Sartre's notion of philosophy (as it is expounded in his *Critique of the Dialectical Reason*) as a way to *totalize* the knowledge of an epoch. Cf. Jean-Paul Sartre, *Critique of the Dialectical Reason*, Vol. 1, trans. by Alan Sheridan-Smith (London: Verso, 2004).

9 Hyppolite's conception of the difference between "philosophers" and "philosophical thought" is in fact compatible with Sartre's idea, expounded in the beginning of the *Critique of Dialectical Reason*, that such thing as "philosophy" does not exist but only philosophers do.

10 This conception of the history of philosophy as *historia perennis*, as a repetition of a limited stock of problems, had been promoted during this period by the Thomist historian of philosophy Etienne Gilson (1884–1978). During the 1950s, Gilson was heavily criticized by Martial Gueroult, starting from the latter's inaugural lecture-manifesto given at the *Collège de France* in 1951 where he succeeded Gilson's chair. Cf. M. Gueroult, *Leçon inaugurale* (Paris: Collège de France, 1951).

CHAPTER SEVEN

Philosophy and ethics[1]

Michel Henry and Alain Badiou

First broadcast: 8 January 1966

[On-screen caption]: "Ethics[2], a normative discipline omnipresent in all philosophical projects"

Michel Henry: It seems very clear to me that one of the problems in answering the question [of the relation between philosophy and ethics] stems from the ambiguity of the world "ethics."

Alain Badiou: Yes, it is obvious that the word "ethics" has many meanings. We could first understand ethics as a particular kind of ethics. This could be something like the set of precepts for carrying out one's life and from this point of view I think you would agree with me in saying that philosophy as such is not in the business of deductively outlining the foundations and justifications of these precepts in detail.

MH: Actually what we traditionally understand by ethics is above all a normative discipline. That is to say, a discipline that aims to assign norms to human actions. But these norms are at the level of the ideal. They are pure significations without a relation with reality. We could say that in this sense ethics cannot to

FIGURE 7.1 *(from left to right)* Badiou, Canguilhem, Ricœur, Dreyfus, Hyppolite. © Centre national de documentation pédagogique

be reduced as such to morality since a norm such as pleasure, defined as the ends of our actions, does not itself create any pleasure in experience and also a norm that we can pose, such as "do one's duty," does not introduce any act which conforms to duty in real experience.

As such, to escape this inevitable difficulty, we should come to a conception of ethics that aims not only to enunciate the norms of reality but to conform to this reality itself and to be itself a moment of life and of existence.

AB: Yes, we might want to put this in order and find concepts in common. We could, it seems to me, distinguish between two different approaches. On the one hand we can consider ethics as defined as a normative discipline and that carries with it a certain number of properly theoretical implications. This is the first way in which it is integrated or very close to philosophy.

MH: Yes, if we consider, for example, Epicurus' ethics of pleasure independently of its normative aspect, we find a presupposed theoretical context. For example, there are needs of different natures. Natural and necessary needs are more easily satisfied and are more easily provided for than others. We should then limit our acts to aim at such needs. Naturally, the theoretical implication of a normative discipline goes very far and we can go further than to say that all normative propositions could, with a modification of sense, be transformed into theoretical propositions. This is why Socrates' ethics is, for example, an ethics attached to the proposition that "no one is voluntarily unethical," a theoretical proposition that means that only the ignorant is unethical and that knowledge distances us from wrongdoing. This means that we should grow in knowledge towards "knowing oneself" precisely in order to act well. And if we look at the description that Kierkegaard gave to this famous thesis in *The Sickness Unto Death*[3] we observe a remarkable discussion. Kierkegaard shows that Socrates is no doubt right in defining ethical failing through ignorance, but nonetheless shows that ethical failing is not the simple privation of knowledge but something rather positive, because he explains that there is a hidden activity of the will that works to obscure knowledge and render ethical failing possible. Regardless of how we evaluate a discussion like this, it is something profoundly philosophical.

AB: But then we could arrive at this first definition. Philosophy has this essential relation with ethics, which is part of it. It most often defined as the path of the theoretical analysis of a certain number of concepts through which the content of normative prescriptions are determined.

MH: Ultimately all disciplines and all normative propositions imply a certain number of fundamental concepts which are philosophical concepts. This seems to be a very important point and we can take, for example, the concept of action[4] and we could conceive of a sort of philosophical purification of ethics that consists in systematically elucidating a theoretical concept that ethics too often uses in an intuitive manner. For example, the concept of action that arises in ethics is most often an intellectualist conception of action that treats action as an objective process and that thinks of action as something blind in itself. It thus needs to produce rules and ends and perhaps ethical norms. And the very idea of a normative ethics is perhaps suspended in this pseudo-concept of action. The same goes for a very classical critique of subjective ethics: this has no meaning unless we think of action as objective.

AB: Yes, but then it seems here that we would lose sight of the core of the debate and the question that I posed to you. It concerned whether ethics has a status within philosophy. It seems to me that if you reduce this attempt of rendering ethics part of philosophy simply from the theoretical implications of normative judgments, you leave it outside of philosophy properly speaking. That is, what is specific to moral judgments and even morality itself is left out. For example, when we say that we should do this rather than something else, naturally there is a complete reflexive determination of this or that in a properly theoretical sense; we agree on this point and we agree that as such it is properly philosophical. Yet the normative form as such, that is to say that the "we should rather" is, in my view, what is specifically ethical in this judgment. And the question is precisely whether we should leave this form itself outside of philosophy.

MH: Yes, in effect if the specificity of ethical activity resides in normative activity, we can ask if this activity is intrinsically philosophical or if it eludes it. I would simply say that in any case, a philosophical question is posed if we reflect on this normative activity. We observe that it cannot hold up norms simply in itself. It is a question of knowing, for example, what norms it would hold up. This is what poses philosophical problems. It would perhaps have to deduce or perhaps induce a norm, in order to legitimate it, from a sort of reading of the whole of human experience. This is philosophical. But there is also another philosophical problem that consists not only in legitimating a particular norm but also in legitimating normative activity as such. Why should there be normative activity as such? That is to say, rather than being spontaneously achieved in itself, why should human activity accept ideal norms as mediations that are perhaps even imposed on it, norms through which it must conform. It is then normativity as such, or even better, a normative and ideal mediation as such that poses a problem and this problem is philosophical.

AB: Yes, but we should be careful, since I fear that there is something in what you say that results in a vicious circle. You say that ethical activity, properly speaking, consists in holding up norms, but we approach philosophy only when we have not only held up these norms but in legitimating these norms that we hold up. So this need for legitimating, this need for a foundation of norms also requires a norm. If we really have this need, it means that we should not hold up these norms unless we are capable of legitimating them. Ethics is then itself omnipresent in the project of philosophy.

MH: In a sense, yes. The need to legitimate normative activity is inscribed in normative activity itself. It only suffices to elucidate it in order to find it so. Normative activity holds up norms that have a value, and thus it asserts a correlate which has a value and which is founded. We thus need this activity to ground itself. That is to say that human beings are not only responsible to norms that it holds up, since we are precisely the ones who hold up these norms. In fact, what is in question here is the responsibility toward the ultimate act of being creators of norms and the creators of ethics. This ultimate responsibility is also a responsibility with regard to the self.

AB: There are two modalities of the presence of ethics in philosophy. There is a presence that I would call thematic – that is, the reflexive and explicit project of founding norms and founding judgments of value regardless of the foundation of this value judgment. And then there is an implicit presence that is hidden and clandestine that is attached to the philosophical project itself. Here I have in mind the beginning of Nietzsche's *Beyond Good and Evil* where Nietzsche basically says that philosophy always defines its project as the search for truth. As such there is a pre-given question that is to know "why truth, why should truth be better than error, why should a project toward truth be held as legitimate? What is the status of truth that has been imposed on philosophers as the object of the search?" And Nietzsche sees it, correctly, there is already something ethical in the philosophical project itself and this brings me to the idea that normative judgments and normative activity are not really specific aspects of human experience, and thus in this way the limits that philosophy places on the domain of ethics perhaps results in something like a loss of a meaning. I would like to give some very simple examples. When I perform an action, it is most of the time animated by a need and a certain number of instruments and tools that are mediators of this action. But these tools are not inert objects and carry in themselves a way in which they are used. These are concrete norms with respect to my action and this presupposes a process of learning and of ideal and intellectual knowledge of the means by which I can appropriate and use these objects. As such I see the presence of a norm at every level of human culture.

I thus see the presence of norms at each level of human culture and the question that I personally ask myself is instead the following one: is the normative activity generally considered as moral not in reality a metamorphosis and perhaps even a distortion of an immediate and concrete normativity that is bequeathed to me by the world, by society, by my environment, in history and practice? In short, is it not an immediate normativity that might be called technico-rational normativity? Well, if we consider any given ethical behavior like that of a mother who wakes up at night with the feeling that she needs to go see her child who is crying, she does this because, as it were, she has the feeling that it is her duty or rather she does this not out of a feeling of an abstract duty but because there is a spontaneous love towards her child. But in reality her behavior to get up, to go to the edge of the crib, to look at her child, to examine, and the like, this behavior is not really due to spontaneous action, it already exists within the status of a model of behavior in the society in which she belongs and the fact that her behavior conforms to this model of behavior seems already to raise up a normative analysis of this social normativity that I evoked a moment ago. I think that the critical examination of normativity in general and moral normativity in particular should thus begin with the examination of this concrete normativity, this technico-rational normativity. Philosophy is not the only project that founds normativity as such since, as I said, this project itself demonstrates a need and, as such, a norm. Philosophy would then be, to take up the vocabulary of Nietzsche, something like a genealogy of morals. That is to say, the study of the aspects, the transformations, and the metamorphoses through which the simple norms of social life and perhaps even of biological life find themselves transformed by a series of procedures that this critique would precisely have to leave behind, in these ideal norms, in these pure norms that we have the habit of considering as moral norms as such. And so, if we raise the problem in this way, we can no longer perhaps respond in ways that you have. We can no longer say that the relation of morality and philosophy is a relation of foundation. It would rather be, in my sense, a relation of critique. Naturally, all critiques tend toward founding, but you see quite clearly in what sense I take this word critique. To critique is to proceed in an analysis of moral value that brings us back to styles of valorization infinitely more immediate and infinitely more empirical and it is thus, in the last instance, nothing but transformation and metamorphosis.

MH: What I want to ask you then is how you conceive of the relation between ethical normativity and this normativity that is much more fundamental and ambiently inscribed in our world.

AB: I would like again to take a concrete or seemingly concrete example. If we try to see how normative categories are progressively interiorized by the child, how the forms of permission and the forbidden come to progressively structure its ideal relation to action, what do we find? We find a certain number of properly technico-rational interdictions, that, for reasons of convenience [*commodité*], parental authority transforms into categorical or universal interdictions: "this is permitted, that is forbidden." Why? Well, because the child is not in a state to understand the explanation that we might give for what is forbidden insofar as it is simply technical or simply rational. It is infinitely more convenient (effective) to have recourse to the original force that the parent has on the child and to use the force of the categories of the permitted and the forbidden. Here we have a sort of universal passage that is exactly the concrete genesis, in short, of ethical normativity, the passage to the universal that has the explication of convenience or, as I would say, the short-circuit of the technico-rational. There are many situations where either we do not want to explain, and these are situations of oppression, or a lot of situations where we cannot explain because, for example, the totality of social structuring is opaque to individual understanding. In any case we see a universal norm of prescription or interdiction emerge that, if we follow the critique to the end, we would in reality see as a technical or practical functioning but that, for its own well-functioning, is given under the form of an ethical universal. And I think that the task of the philosophy and its variably direct and indirect relation to ethical life is to elucidate the process of this metamorphosis and to refer back to this apparently trans-historical universality of ethical norms to its ultimate foundation, which is the systematic totality of culture[5] considered as a true historical transcendental.[6]

MH: Yes, but even so I have two questions. What you have given an account for here is a necessary appearance, in the mind of the child, of a universalizable and universalized interdiction. The problem would be to know if its characteristics allow us to sufficiently define an interdiction and a moral obligation. That is to say that in the moment when you make this inevitable mystification in the mind of a child, the ethicist recognizes something like moral conscience or a conscience distinguished from ethics. That is to say that in moral conscience, if we believe the descriptions of ethicists, there is a sort of autonomy that you have not accounted for.[7] There is still something more, that is, the specific phenomenological character specific to ethical values which you might not be taking into consideration. I see that the conscience of the child is exactly like the conscience of an adult. But what I absolutely disagree with you on is the very nature of your explication precisely because it is an explication. I do not believe in explications, that is to say, an explication which starts from a certain number of objective determinations as premises and from which we think we can come to, as a solution, a certain subjective structure, that is, the structure of conscious morality. For me, the premises and the conclusion come from heterogeneous dimensions and in order to go from the one to the other we need to make a leap that renders all explication of a subjective structure an objective one, the trace of an insurmountable contingency.[8] This means that we must somehow believe in this explication regardless of how interesting it may be. No doubt reductions of this form that attempts at a subjective structure from the basis of objective antecedents are very numerous. There are reductions not only like the one you have proposed but there are certainly also psychoanalytic reductions, sociological reductions, and certainly biological reductions. This means that I am equally bothered by the fact that your explication is not the only one that makes this leap and that requires us, at the end of a day, to believe.

AB: So then you completely reject the possibility of similar reductions?

MH: Oh no! Not at all, not at all! What I say is that this reduction would be truly assured if it would be possible to ground it phenomenologically. That is to say that if we wish to show that this lacking concrete norm is lived as a lack and that it thus motivates, if you like, the emergence of an absolutely new intentionality that we need to take into account, it poses a normativity that is in this case of a different order than the ethical.

AB: But not at all, not at all! If a transformed norm can function like an efficacious illusion, it is precisely because its concrete functioning is not lived in the transparency and the knot of explication is found there. I take up my silly example a moment ago of the woman who gets up in the middle of the night to check on her child. We understand that she is not clearly conscious of the grounds of the acquired behavior or the cultural model of the norm to which her action conforms. If she was really aware of this she would find her actions encumbered and quasi-paralysed, and that is to say that inasmuch as she has an absolute awareness of this norm [no], she has the awareness of conforming to what she *should* do. We then have at the same time a living of a norm that phenomenology can describe and, on the other hand, a concrete foundation of the norm that the critique or genealogy should also describe. I don't see an incompatibility here.

MH: All the same, if the founding activity of these technical significations that you recognize exists and if it could be that this activity is comprehensible in itself with respect to intentionality, then one of the following things must be the case. Either these concrete norms represents the final ground of our experience and its foundation, the basis from which everything in our experience is explained, or instead there is something more fundamental in which concrete norms themselves are rooted. Why do we not say that? You say that these are technical norms, that is to say, the norms on which actions are modeled, but you forbid grasping action through what is anterior to these given concrete norms. You have given the example of this woman. That is all well. We admit that there is no historical moment anterior to this technico-cultural information but nonetheless there is something foundationally anterior, it is the fact of this activity that informs these norms. This activity is first that of existence, I mean that it is not determined by the context which is always a consequence of it but rather determined by the subjective structure of existence insofar as practical existence, not in terms of ethical existence but that of an active existence. It is only through the fundamental structure of active existence that this world of technique and culture comes to take shape in its own way.

[On-screen caption]: "Ethical normative activity, a system founded on an absolute and concrete subjectivity"

AB: I would say that we both admit that there are historically given structures through which normative activity can be thought and reduced, not totally, not founded and restrained, but in any case …

MH: Ethical normative activity.

AB: Yes, absolute but *concrete*.

MH: For my part, I agree with you but in simply adding the following. For me, we can draw nothing from this absolute subjectivity in the order of knowledge, even if it is perhaps founded in the order of being, an effective intelligibility in the historical *a priori* that it supports.

Notes

1   This interview has never been transcribed and edited. One might conjecture that this is due to Badiou and Henry's profound disagreements. Curiously enough, in 1966 Alain Badiou will dedicate a series of lectures to ethics at the University of Reims entitled *Les invariants du moralisme: Bergson, Gide, Sartre* [The invariants of moralism: Bergson, Gide, Sartre].

2   The French title of this interview was *"Philosophie et morale."* In French *"morale"* and *"éthique"* have slightly different meanings. The term *"éthique"* refers to contingent or localized norms produced "immanently" by action which may correspond more to the English use of the Latin *"ethos."* The term *"morale"* refers to the transcendent norms regulating action or the norms held as ideal, universal, or eternal. In translation, we have consistently rendered the word *"morale"* as "ethics" which corresponds more closely with the current English understanding of a normative discipline. The translation of *"moralité,"* *"ethique"* and other normative terms are rendered differently according to context.

3   Soren Kierkegaard, *The Sickness Unto Death: A Christian Psychological Exposition For Upbuilding And Awakening*, trans. by Howard and Edna H. Hong (Princeton: Princeton University Press, 1983). Henry focused some of his commentary on this book in his primary Ph.D. dissertation *The Essence of the Manifestation*. Cf. Michel Henry, *The Essence of Manifestation*, trans. by Girard Etzkorn (The Hague: Martinus Nijhoff, 1973), 476. Henry then comments on Kierkegaard's *The Concept of Dread* in his second Ph.D. dissertation *Philosophy and Phenomenology of the Body*. Cf. *Michel Henry, Philosophy and Phenomenology of the Body, trans.* by Girard J, Etzkorn (The Hague: Martinus Nijhoff, 1975). Cf. Soren Kierkegaard, The Concept of Dread, trans. by W. Lowrie (Princeton: Princeton University Press, 1957).

4   This concept is carefully examined and criticized in both of Michel Henry's dissertations.

5   Here Badiou's position seems similar to the ones expressed by the two founders of modern sociology, Emile Durkheim and Lucien Lévy-Bruhl, made current in the context of the 1960s by Pierre Bourdieu.

6   The concept of a "historical transcendental" or, more precisely, a "historical *a priori*" had been introduced by Edmund Husserl in the texts surrounding his 1936 *Crisis of European Sciences and*

Transcendental Philosophy to solve the problem of the relation between the concrete *a priori* and the historical sense of scientific knowledge. Husserl had introduced this concept in his famous text "The Origin of Geometry." This was partially translated by Paul Ricoeur during the 1930s and then completely translated and introduced in a volume by Jacques Derrida in 1962. Cf. Edmund Husserl, *L'origine de la géometrie*, trans. and ed. by Jacques Derrida (Paris: PUF, 1962). Michel Foucault used this term in his first book, *Maladie mentale et personnalité* (1954), then in *Madness and Civilization* (1962), in *The Birth of the Clinic* (1963), and finally in *The Order of Things* (1966), where it is defined as the field of organization of a possible knowledge.

7 Henry defends what he calls the "formal structure of autonomy" in *The Essence of Manifestation*. Michel Henry, *The Essence of Manifestation*, 220.

8 The category of contingency used by Henry in both of his two Ph.D. dissertations is a key concept in French existentialist phenomenology since Sartre.

CHAPTER EIGHT

Model and structure

Michel Serres and Alain Badiou

First broadcast: 9, 16, and 23 January 1968 [three parts][1]

[Start of *Modèle et Structure partie II*]

Michel Serres: It is clear that in the many sciences, the applied sciences, the sciences of nature, biology, and technology also …

Alain Badiou: … the human sciences.[2]

MS: Yes, the human sciences also. We are led towards the construction of models.[3] What is the sense of models in these cases? We might hold up the following definition: we construct a model when we construct a theoretical schema, or following the distinctions we visited a moment ago, an abstract schema, or when we construct an apparatus or any sort of object that simulates, imitates, or analogically represents a given phenomenon with parameters that would otherwise be difficult to determine in a direct manner. As such, we will have constructed a model that would be, in a certain manner, a *metaxu*, that is to say, an inter-mediate between a theoretical field belonging to some scientific inquiry and a phenomenon from that field.[4]

AB: Would you then admit the following figural representation or schematic model? We have on one side, the object or the object to be known and on the other, the theoretical field that this object is supposed to open up.

MS: Yes.

AB: However, we would not be in a position to establish a control, a direct determination [*maîtrise directe*] of the theoretical field with respect to the object.

MS: Perfectly right.

AB: The theory cannot appropriate the object. This supposed object is a phenomenon that has certain effects which are ultimately determinable as processes. Hence we have the object, its effects and the theoretical field but there is no direct relation. We would thus be constructing, if we can put it this way, something between the theoretical field and the indeterminate or relatively indeterminate object. We would be constructing an intermediate object, a model, controlled by the theoretical field, which would, in its turn, have certain effects and the theoretical control over the model that permits one to obtain a level of effects, a correspondence, an analogy, indirect or detached but which finally permits us to establish a sort of indirect control, a mediate control, of the initial object. Would you agree?

MS: Yes, I would. And, if you want, in nuance, the analogy between the obtained effects by means of the model and the expected or known effects of the phenomena under investigation would serve to maintain the fidelity [*fidélité*] of the model. When I employ the term "fidelity" I am using it in the Leibnizian sense. Leibniz used the term "fidelity" in the same sense.[5]

AB: What I would add is that the construction of such an intermediate model would not only serve in the theoretical determination of an indeterminate object, or one with too many parameters to be directly or immediately determined, but can also prepare us for practical or technical interventions on certain phenomena.

MS: It is this distinction that I would like to bring to my definition. That is to say that my definition remains valid not only for the explication of phenomena that remain difficult to theoretically determine but also for interventions on this phenomenon. I will take an example. Everyone knows that there are catastrophic floods on the river Garonne.[6]

[Film montage of the river Garonne flooding]

Well, given this natural phenomenon that is not theoretically understood but that we (also) do not have under control, praxically speaking, the anxious public authorities have trusted the *Chatou* laboratory, specialists in hydrodynamics, to study the problem. At the laboratory, one has a constructed model, a sort of object that is a reduced model of a section of the riverbed of the Garonne through which we can experiment on the flow of the Garonne and the effects in question. Once we have an experiment on these effects on a reduced model, this simulated working model [*maquette*], one is ready to work against the possible catastrophes by measuring the points of impact, the weak points of the circulation of water. Thus we have here a reduced model, a working model for intervention.

[Film montage of the laboratory showing researchers working with experiments in running water through a reduced model of the geographic region]

AB: I think we are ready for a second definition of model. That is, we might perhaps also adopt another point of view. We have basically defined a model with respect to something other than itself; either with the structure of which it is the model or the object for which it is a model. But might we turn to an internal form of a model, if I might put it without too much of a play on words, one could "insert" into the structure of model and define a typology on this basis; a different typology. The typology I propose is the following. It seems that one can distinguish between theoretical models, schemas, diagrams, and apparatuses. So it seems that, to continue to break down our examples from a moment ago, we can proceed in the following fashion. A theoretical model can be taken in two senses. It's hard to miss them. First, a model may be part of an abstract structure containing various models. However, there is also a sense in which a conceptual structure can serve to model something that has an unassignable reality. This is the case, for example, with the celebrated cosmological models, the models of the universe.

[Film montage of ancient cosmological models, Chaldean, Egyptian, and Chinese]

AB: So far as schemas are concerned, for example, we can take the organizational chart [*organigramme*] of a large administration.

[Film montage of an organizational chart on paper]

AB: We see that such an apparatus is a schema in the sense that it gives a geometric representation of something that is not necessarily geometric. Also, there are apparatuses, automata [*automata*], the assemblage of materials that permits us to obtain either a simulation or an imitation, or in any case a correspondence on the level of effect and function.

[Film montage of small-scale mechanical machines]

I think that covers the field.

MS: I completely agree and that is quite interesting not only because it highlights many good points and permits a sort of encyclopaedic sweep of the notion but also because it goes from the most abstract to the most concrete. That is to say that in the case of theoretical models we will have abstract models, as is the case for the models of the universe. On the other hand, for what concerns the apparatuses or the artefacts we will have models of concretization. I am completely in agreement with your view.

AB: You have unfolded an ordering in my schema. We might, I think, give some examples for each case, because it seems to me to be epistemologically indispensable. In the case of logico-mathematical models, a first signification of the theoretical model is the structure of groups. What is interesting is that in

traversing this pair "model-structure," we get a sort of relativi-
sation of the pair "abstract-concrete." When we talk about
the structure of a group having the transformation group of
Euclidian space as a model, for example, it can hardly be called
"concrete" in the basic sense of the term. It is as if in these
cases, we have a stratification of terms with the pair "structure-
model," that an abstract structure with models can always in
turn be held as the model of a structure at a higher stratum.

MS: Not always …

AB: Not always but for some cases, a good number of cases.

MS: Certainly. Outside the logico-mathematical field, we can
gather some senses of the term "model" from physical and
biological sciences. Certain theorists speak of the model of
the "valve." They mean to say that there are relations which
are valid in one direction but not in another direction. This
functions, then, like a valve. For example, a semi-conductor is a
valve. In certain chemical reactions we need a catalyst that acts
in one direction but not in the other. I think that the example
that strikes me as being the most brilliant at present can be
drawn from an exciting field of science that is so absolutely on
the advance, that is to say, the science of macromolecules. This
field that has won so many the Nobel prizes in recent years. We
now often speak of the "key and lock" model in this science.
What is interesting is that certain authors, instead of speaking
of the key-lock, call it the model of a "mould-cast." But what
does this really mean? It reminds me of a Latin expression, the
"*tessera*."[7] What is the "key-lock" model? The key-lock model
functions in the following way. Certain complex chemical
groups make up a part of a greater biochemical molecule. The
scientific field of biochemistry has been concentrating itself
here. We have a macromolecule that possesses certain complex
chemical bonds, these chemical bonds are at work in an elective
or in an absolutely preferential way over the chemical bonds
of another macromolecule. Biochemists call this a key and lock
precisely because of this selection of molecules or preferential
configuration. This functions like a key that corresponds with a
lock that it meets. Clearly, we have something like a deprived or

rustic model here. To understand this a little more, we can call on the notion of information. A piece of information is carried by the design of the key and it corresponds to the keyhole in question. What is interesting about the key-lock model is that it is applicable to so many cases and many that are to be considered under an ordering structure [*structure d'ordre*]. For example, one such case is the synthesis of deoxyribonucleic acid (DNA)[8]; another case where one finds the key-lock model is in the synthesis of ribonucleic acid (RNA). A third case of the same key-lock phenomenon is the key-lock model in the synthesis of proteins. But instead of the key-lock model working only once, say, in the synthesis of DNA or uniquely in what concerns the synthesis of RNA or in the synthesis of protein, the key-lock phenomenon or the key-lock model poses further complexities with additional mechanisms in what biochemists have called a "zipper," which is to say that there is a repetition of processes such that the function of protein synthesis can be compared to a zipper. You understand that we cannot enter into the details for a complete exposé of this here and ...

AB: Yes, but I would like you to remark on something. We are in the course of explaining theoretical models. We agree on this.

MS: That's right.

AB: But there might be confusions in the minds of those who are listening or watching us because these models, called valves, key-lock, and zipper are all clearly concrete images.

MS: I want to respond to this because it is quite important. Here we have the impression, as you say, that the abstract phenomenon becomes precisely a concrete model. It is clear that when speaking of the pair "key-lock" or the "mould-cast" or the zipper, of which we have been speaking – these are manners of speaking concretely. But what it hides is, in fact, the abstract relations of which the cases indicated are applications.

AB: I suppose then that when you speak of a valve you are simply designating an irreversible relation, which is really something effectively theoretical.

MS: Yes, that's right. If you like, we might call these models, the valve models, the lock models, or mould-cast models, I would like to call these "blind" structures. That is to say that these are very much models in the scientific sense but in fact, for the rest of us, us philosophers, these are all structures in a certain manner, structures that one might call blind insofar as we model them. But what is more exciting in this phenomenon is the repetition of key-lock model to be found in the phenomenon of the duplication of chromosomes, in the function of nerve-synapses, in a lot of other phenomena. We find the repetition of this blind structure in increasingly complicated ways in a series of biological phenomena which had not previously been conceived as having such a relation. It is clear that the great invention of contemporary biochemistry is the grouping of phenomena under this "skeleton key" [*clef de voûte*] that is this key-lock phenomenon.

AB: I think that it is impossible to evoke the theoretical model without making mention of the cosmological models as they are some of the most ancient and thus most worthy [*digné*] in a certain regard. Basically since Anaximander, and since the dawn of Greek thought, we are in a position to say that there existed a conceptual model of the universe.

MS: I think that it is necessary to introduce some finer distinctions. In the epoch of Anaximander, that is to say, the physicists of Miletus, there existed, effectively, a model of the universe. Yet, in that case, it is rather more of a schema, a theoretical schema in contrast to the case of the model of the universe conceived by Archimedes. We certainly know that Archimedes, or his students, built an artificial construction. First, we have the case of the theoretical model, which is to say, the schema of the universe; in the second, an artificial representation of this same universe. However, one can make an even finer distinction there because we have cases where the model of the universe is not only a theoretical schema or an artefact, that is to say, a representation or an object that represents the world. There is also the case where the schema is complicated by other consid-erations, of astrology, magic, or religion, such as we see in the "Mysterium Cosmographicum" of Kepler, where one effectively has a model of the world from a theoretical schema, according to which it has been rigorously constructed, while on the other hand, it is mixed with considerations of harmonics, and even music. As such we have a very complex model.

AB: A sort of model that is in some way saturated with references to structures belonging to different theoretical registers ...

MS: Yes, that's right.

AB: ... to different theoretical spaces.

MS: So the case of Kepler is probably the most overloaded case. The case of Anaximander would probably be a pure case. The case of Archimedes would be an intermediate case where one would have, at the same time, a theoretical schema and its realization in an object.

AB: Basically, in the case of the models of the universe in contemporary science or contemporary cosmology, one remains in the legacy of Anaximander, because the foundation of these models is the identification of a universal space: a real space, a mathematical space, a geometric space. That is why we might speak of a Euclidian model of the universe and a non-Euclidian model of the universe. Furthermore, since it is not a matter of cosmology but of *cosmogony*, when one considers the entire process which results in the state of the universe, we might even, from an interpretation of the Doppler effect in terms of expansion, imagine, for example, a model of the universe where expansion is continuous after an initial point of concentration. For example, we can turn to the hypothesis of a primeval atom formulated by Georges Lemaître [*L'Abbé lemaître*], or we might construct an oscillating model where expansion is only a phase where, after reaching a certain degree of maximum expansion and equilibrium, it is followed by a phase of contraction or retraction. In these cases, we have pure models at work. They are purely theoretical because, having introduced the initial hypotheses, they are developed in a strictly mathematical fashion.

MS: Here, we can also make a distinction; tell me what you think of the following. In general, a model, probably also in the case of a model of the universe, is the meeting place of hypotheses and, in the case of the universe in expansion where we consider the phenomenon of the Doppler effect, we have the idea of a certain selection of hypotheses. Everything happens through the choice of a preferential hypothesis from which to develop the model. Thus there would be, in this case, models that are more laden with hypotheses than others and so forth. In all rigorousness, one might make this distinction as well, I think.

AB: The grouping of hypotheses, the selection of hypotheses. Yes, I think that one can retain this distinction. Well then, I think that we might return to our initial typology. There are, following from this, schemas. There are schemas, there are diagrams, and there are graphic representations of some relations which are not necessarily geometric. You had some good examples of these.

MS: It is clear that with this type, the examples abound. It is good to recall – I believe it should be familiar to the students of the senior year of high school [*classe terminale*] – the famous example of (Niels) Bohr's atom. This famous Bohr atom schematizes the atom according to a planetary model with a central nucleus and electrons in the periphery orbit. That is to say, the atom is formed in the manner of the solar system in miniature. The problem is that it is necessary to know what degree of confidence to accord to this type of model. In the case of Bohr's atom, we have an especially clear case. From the beginning, that is to say, from the moment when we had put this planetary schema, this solar system, into place, physicists had a limited degree of confidence in the model, which then permitted the unleashing of scientific research in this direction. We reached a point where Bohr's atom, which was a union of hypotheses and which transferred the cosmological model on the problem of the atom, developed towards the erasure of the planetary orbit of peripheral atoms, at the moment when wave mechanics came onto the scene. At this moment, we understood that the linear orbit of the peripheral electron was probably imaginary or a vague intuition and we will not be any worse off if we replaced it with what can be called the continuous distribution of the probability of the electron's presence.

AB: This is what Bachelard called the shading in [*estompage*] of the orbit.[9]

MS: Yes. In the contemporary textbooks which speak of Bohr's schema, we get the sense that the orbit has been shaded with a greyish coloured tint. But at the same time, we see how the model developed by Bohr evolved. We know that there are other examples not taken from the physics or theoretical schema of this order. An example might be chosen from chemistry. A well-known formula which has been of great importance to the epistemological development of chemistry is the famous development of the core of Benzene by (August) Kekulé – you know, the distribution of atoms in a hexagonal schema for the chemistry of aromatic isomers. This model is particularly precious in the evolution of chemistry with respect to these lines, called the valences, which were not very understood. But what happened was that, possibly contrary to the case of Bohr's schema, once the chemists applied a measure to the distance or the angles of the valences, the schema became a considerable catalyst for the exploration of the depths of the material itself.[10]

AB: It seems to me that we are running a bit out of time for the exploration of the model of the apparatus, the artificial apparatus, the artefact, but we might treat three proper epistemic problems from what you just suggested. The first of these problems would be the importation of concepts in the construction of models, because we were speaking about Bohr's model whose origins were not immediately physical but cosmological. The second is the model as an obstacle, as you said yourself, that it was necessary to undo certain aspects internal to the organization of Bohr's model. And, thirdly, it is the positive or catalytic function that the model fulfills, in the cases that you just evoked.

MS: I think we should, with respect to the three problems, evoke issues concerning their evolution and their utilization. I would like to go back to a precise point. In the case of schemas, I first took the planetary representation of Bohr's atom as an example and then I took the molecular representation of Kekulé and I would try to complete this, since we have passed from atom to molecule and from molecule to crystal by the crystallographic [*crystallographique*][11] network, which is equally a schema which represents, analogically, a conception of matter. So I think that it is important to recognize that there are atomic models, molecular models, and crystalline models. And, we have models that function better or worse at each stage of this scale and so forth. Even more than this physical-chemical hierarchy, I would add that since we have been treating schemas or schematic models, that schematic models are not only physical-chemical. In effect, we were speaking a while ago about the *organigramme*, the organizational chart, the chart of the administrative organization, the organization of the service of a factory; we have a schema that makes visible the distribution of authority. But this schema, in my sense, is a graph and that should be distinguished from other schemas employed in the same sense. For instance, it is possible to create a schema of the telephone installation or the network in an *arrondissment* of Paris. We are in the presence here of two graphs[12] of which, in the first case, very specifically, carries out a law (*porteur d'une loi*). On the graph, we can read the law of the distribution of authority of the group in question. In the second case, we have a graph that does not represent a law but rather represents something that is materially constituted by the telephone lines themselves. As such, we have a representative graph in the first case, and in the other case, a theoretical graph. Here, the first model is the carrying out of a law and the second model is the carrying out, we might say, of a representation.

AB: Thus might we not tie this distinction to our proposition by remarking that, in the case of the *organigramme*, the organizational chart of the administration which allows us to directly read off the hierarchical order, a structure is given, an ordering structure? What characterizes the diagram of the telephone lines is that it is a diagram where all the segments are reversible and where one does not read off any structure.

MS: Certainly.

AB: Thus we might then say that a graph is a model if one can immediately read off the principle of ordering insofar as the graph is a structured graph with an ordering structure. By contrast, if we have a representative graph, we will not discover any structure at all except for the tracing of the composition that it is representative of.

[End of *Modèle et Structure partie II*]

[Start of *Modèle et Structure partie III*]

AB: We might return with some stubbornness to the epistemological questions posed before: obstacle, catalyst, the importation of concepts. We should treat these questions (a little further). We have spoken of the model as obstacle apropos of Bohr's atom which has become, thanks to Bachelard[13], a canonical example of the image of an obstacle. If we were to summarize all this, we could say that the model as a theoretical figure or as a theoretical image can have an ambiguous function. What Bachelard showed very clearly was that this model could be an intuitive support that sustains a progressive structural investigation, but the excessive materialization of orbits, a way of taking the finite model too seriously, can be, in a strict sense, an obstacle to the progress of a structural investigation such that the reworking of the mathematic structure operates by taking into account the effacement of certain of the relations within the figure as opposed to taking its evidence from the figure itself. One might say that the graph is a concretization of a structure but the progress and the reworking of the structure itself implies, at the same time, a de-concretization of the model.

MS: That is very true. I would like to bring up an image from an English physicist, I don't remember which, who said that a model that is, little by little, effaced for the sake of a theoretical schema resembles a cat effaced for the sake of its smile.

AB: I believe that you have also evoked, with respect to the image, a scaffolding, or more precisely a cement cast. When the cement is set, the cast can be removed.

MS: That's right. I wanted to look at this case and I would like, in response to your first question, which is about the obstacle, to say that models are also catalysts. I mean by this an epistemological situation in the following: at the cutting edge of science, I mean the precise point when science is the most alive, the most subtle and the most detailed models abound. Every time one discovers a new particle, we are in a place to imagine new models. In the nineteenth century it was very much the case with respect to the thermodynamics of gases. Lord Kelvin spoke of red spheres that he observed vibrate in the atmosphere or in a liquid in question.

AB: A fluid ...

MS: A fluid, exactly. As a science advances, we have a large plurality of models, it is clear that to find a law for developing these models, the problem is ... well, we could rather say that a first counter-example would burst this "trial balloon" [*ballon d'essai*].[14] That is to say that at the cutting edge where we have this great number of models, which are trial balloons insofar as there are many hypotheses, the first counter-example would puncture a balloon and the only criterion to use to perceive the success of the model is where the model survives. It gives way to the theoretical schema. In this way, we can say that the successful model functions with respect to a theory like a scaffolding or a cement cast, as you said just before. That is to say, one raises a sort of schema, an object, or an artefact, and one transforms it by filling the vague intuition with a mathematical reality. Thus when the mathematical schema is organized, we remove the intuitive cast and there remains the mathematical construction which allows us to directly determine the phenomenon. By consequence, the first criterion is the survival (of the model) and the second criterion is the continuous progress of the model and its final disappearance. Here, I want to insist on two other points. The first is the fidelity of models. Clearly, a model is only as good as its fidelity. We resume what we were saying before when we said that given the character and determination of an object under study and the character or determination of the model, the whole problem consists in rendering the richest possible intersection between the two. I said just now that the only criterion for a good model is its survival. Is there a critical principle behind this criterion? The critical principle, in my sense, would be the following. Sometimes, in order to understand a given phenomenon, we bring it under models which come from a theoretical field different than the phenomenon being studied. For example, we have electric models, electronic models, models coming from information theory [*theorie d'information*], for a certain number of organic phenomena.[15]

AB: Also, we find linguistic models for certain ethnographic phenomena.

MS: For example, with what concerns synaptic contact, we have a certain number of models. The problem that I consider most pressing is the following. Do we have the right and under what conditions can we effectively import a certain concept from another theoretical space into another theoretical field?[16] I believe that it is a fundamental question concerning the methodology surrounding the use of models. We do not really have a solution to this right away but it is a point that I think we should continue to work on.

AB: This critical question, the question of the right or the legitimacy of importing concepts from a theoretical region that is not that of the object of study. This question is profound and important but I am not sure that we can find a response to this question this evening. I don't know what you think of this.

MS: Yes, neither this evening nor the next morning probably. But what I do want to say with regards to this is the following. We said earlier that, at the cutting edge of a science, there is a large amount of models. This may help us to describe the phenomenon that we are discussing. It happens sometimes that when we switch from thinking about a particular field of science to the totality of science, or at least of a wider region, that suddenly, on the occasion of an important discovery or a strong global hypothesis, a science advances over other fields. At this delicate point, there arise a great number of models, and these models refigure themselves through the course of inquiry like an eruption over the totality of neighbouring fields. We had examples of such a phenomenon in the first part of this century with the importance of information theory. The concepts were still blurry and there are such a great number of models but suddenly, in examples from physics and chemistry and in examples from biochemistry, we find these concepts emanating and being utilized in other domains of theory. This phenomenon is one of quantitative importation.

AB: But, you see, I was just thinking that, when you posed this critical question, I was thinking of a comparable phenomenon in the field of the human sciences, because it is clear that the field of linguistics, since the beginning of the century, has been given the charge of the refiguring of the form of science [*la forme de la scienticité*]. And what happened was that it gave way to a massive exportation of concepts such that it appears to be taken in its totality as the scientific model of all others. Linguistics is a science that has been taken as a model for the other sciences, a science that is the theoretical region from which one exports a whole series of concepts.

MS: The supplier of models ...

AB: Yes, the great supplier of models. I think that in this field the question of legitimacy is really an epistemological question that characterizes modernity. I am thinking, for example, of ethnology or the structural analysis of folklore that have been undertaken by the Russian formalist school.[17] What happens in all this? What is borrowed is the idea of the dissection [*découpage*] of a corpus into pertinent unities in taking the dissection of the (grammatical) chain as a model, by the "the" [*le*], or the irreducible and indecomposable elements (of language) linked by their pertinent oppositions, the phonemes. For example, Levi-Strauss undertakes an analysis of myth where he reserves the necessity of dissecting the narrative of a text of myth and its variations into a certain number of structural elements that are indecomposable and which are called, precisely, "mythemes."

[Film montage of a reading from the discussion of Oedipus from chapter ten of Lévi-Strauss' *Structural Anthropology*[18]]

AB: This is a second operation which shows to what point linguistics functions as a model for the borrowing of groups of morphisms, an operation that ties together these dissected elements. In taking linguistics as a model, one attributes an extreme importance to the notion of the pairs of oppositions such that mythemes are defined, like a phoneme, only through their oppositions with the others. Like the phoneme, nothing but the articulation of oppositions allow for its determination. Ultimately, we investigate, in traversing the series, all the myth's or the text's variants by utilizing its various transformations. We look for an invariant structure in the context of a surprising or even equivocal concept of the model. Or rather, we might say that the structural invariant that we would have constructed would be the following. For example, in taking the myth of Oedipus, all the variations of the myth of Oedipus are understood by Lévi-Strauss through the Oedipus complex as described by Freud. We would say here that the invariant of the variations is a constructed model. But fundamentally, we could rather say that we have therefore opened up a structure where all the particular myths of the series are models. Well, it seems that by traversing this series of operations that characterizes the modern epistemic field, the question of legitimacy is quite sharply posed. It is posed on the level of the relevance of the unities when we operate by this dissection because, in linguistics, there is a control afforded by the meaning of speech. When one operates a substitution of phonemes, the listener may or may not receive decipherable information. It is clear that in the case of myth, there is a question of whether a dissection in terms of the various morphisms obtains an invariant in the operation of the series, that is, whether one can say when and if there is a true invariant. This is the question of legitimacy that is left open. Ultimately, it is only to be distinguished, in my opinion, by an inaugural postulate, by the importation of a concept, or an affirmation that a myth is structured like a language. That is, can we pronounce, along with Lacan taken as a structuralist psychologist, the inaugural assertion? That what? That the unconscious is structured like a language.[19] There, we are at the heart of the epistemological difficulty that was raised because of the importation of concepts. It becomes, finally, in itself, a first axiom that constitutes the legitimacy of the whole theoretical enterprise.

MS: It becomes even more certain through your assertions that mythology or the unconscious is structured like a language insofar as we get the impression that the most important part of these aphorisms is the term "like" [*comme*]. Precisely in the prehistory of the notion of "model," as the epistemologist Pierre Duhem[20] began to philosophically elucidate, it is in this question or in this methodology of models that we encounter a philosophical horizon which is dominated by the philosophy of "as if" [*comme si*]. Thus, we might be in the same philosophical situation. Something happens "like" something and this is a methodology from models.

AB: I wonder whether the question posed by this philosophical-epistemological problem which concerns this permanent reference to the "as if" is always apparent, given all the shifts and possible slippage [*glissement*] of meaning from a rigorous to a devaluated sense of the word "structure" we just spoke of, or even in considering the archaic senses of the term. Concerning structuralism in literary criticism, I would, if you like, approach this field to take into account the risk taken by the usage of the epistemic pair of structure and model.

MS: We should say that, so far as literary criticism is concerned, when we speak of a structural critique or structuralism, it is often that terms are taken in their devalued sense, in a sense that was scrutinized at the beginning (the first part) of this program.[21] As such, frequently, when the critic discovers, in a text or a novel or a piece of theatre, a rigorous organization of the field, he will declare that he is doing a structural investigation. This is not quite evident.

AB: I think we can return to saying that the discovery of an organization or an arrangement is not a structural discovery even if this organization is given to being more or less formalized. I think this precaution is indispensible. Or rather, not all formalism has the right to declare itself structuralist. From a different point of view, we are not really applying a structural methodology even if the criticism possesses a dissection of a certain number of themes that are systematically organized. That is, even if we have, as expressed by (the work of) Henri Michaux, what might be called the imaginary universe of an author.[22] Otherwise put, a structural critique is neither purely nor simply a structuralist critique nor in any case a thematic critique.

MS: I quite agree on this point.

AB: But the question presupposes knowledge of what a structural critique is!

MS: It seems to me that, in this case, it would do us well to demonstrate movement by actually walking. I want to propose a structural or structuralist critique of a well-known text, *Dom Juan* by Molière.[23] You probably know, having read the *"Essai sur le don"* of Marcel Mauss, the law of gift exchange [*l'échange des dons*].[24] I think that this law is probably at work in *Dom Juan* of Molière. Whether Molière had this in mind or not is not my question. I would say, however, that romanticism took up the figure of Dom Juan as a sort of hero or a psychoanalytically empathetic hero, that is to say, in his being a ladies-man [*homme à femmes*]. In Molière's *Dom Juan*, it seems to me that the notion of hero is much richer and his behavior is precisely definable by paying attention to a certain number of things.

First, we see that Dom Juan does not pay his debts – I'll return to this later. There is then some behavior regarding money. On the other hand, we find his classic behavior, as we know, with respect to women. Finally, there is also behavior particularly with respect to words, with taking oaths, promise-making, and so on. As such, it would be interesting to compare the schema of Dom Juan with respect to words, motivations like money and also women. We can also add here the consideration of life, which we will speak of in a moment. I would say that the behavior of Dom Juan with regard to words and women and motivators follows the law of gift exchange that we mentioned earlier. I will get back to this, but what is it that we find in the opening of the text of *Dom Juan*?

We can read in the opening section of *Dom Juan* a curious praise of tobacco. So I take this praise of tobacco as a model and it is very precisely a reduced model of Dom Juan's actions with respect to the three things. Tobacco is praised in the following way. When one has tobacco and offers the tobacco, the other person accepts the tobacco when it is offered and hence tobacco is an element that follows the law of gift exchange. But very curiously as we follow the passage, on the question of tobacco,

Molière writes that, "anyone who is able to live without it …"
– I don't remember …

AB: "… is unworthy to draw breath."[25]

MS: "… is unworthy to draw breath." Here, I translate that he who does not accept the law of gift exchange through tobacco is one who loves death.

[Excerpt from the film *Dom Juan* by the director Marcel Blüwal[26]: Act 1, scene 1]

SGANARELLE: [holding a snuffbox in his hand]. I don't care what Aristotle and the philosophers say: there's nothing in this world like snuff. All right-minded people adore it; and anyone who is able to live without it is unworthy to draw breath. It not only clears and delights the brain; but it also inclines the heart towards virtue, and helps one to become a gentleman. Haven't you noticed how, as soon as one begins to take it, one becomes uncommonly generous to everybody, ready to present one's box right and left wherever one goes?[27] [End of excerpt]

MS: As I have said, this is a reduced model. We give and exchange through tobacco, et cetera. We see the behavior of Dom Juan with regard to money in three scenes in particular. There is the final scene where Sganarelle demands the wages that Dom Juan had not paid him.

[Excerpt of Act 5, scene 6]

SGANARELLE: Oh my wages, my wages! By his death everyone is satisfied … Everyone is content. I am the only one to suffer, I who after so many years' service have no other reward than that of seeing with my own eyes my master's impious behavior punished by the most horrible punishment imaginable. But who will pay my wages?[28] [End of excerpt]

MS: There is also the famous scene with Mr Dimanche where he refuses to pay Mr Dimanche.

[Excerpt of Act 4, scenes 2 and 3]

LA VIOLETTE: Sir, Monsieur Dimanche the shopkeeper is asking to speak to you.

SGANARELLE: That's splendid! All we needed was a creditor to come and dun us for money. What does he mean by coming here asking for money? Why didn't you tell him that the master wasn't at home?

LA VIOLETTE: I have been telling him so for the last three-quarters of an hour, but he won't believe it. He's sitting down there, inside the door waiting.

SGANARELLE: Then let him wait.

DON JUAN: No, on the contrary, tell him to come up. It's bad policy to hide oneself from creditors. They must be paid with something. I know the way to send them away satisfied without giving them a penny.

[*Enter* M. DIMANCHE]

Ah, come in, Monsieur Dimanche. I am delighted to see you. My rascals shall smart for not letting you up at once. It's true that I had given orders that no one was to be admitted but that was not meant for you. My door will always be open to you.

M. DIMANCHE: I am humbly obliged to you, Sir.

DON JUAN: [*to* LA VIOLETTE *and* RAGOTIN] Dammit, you rogues, I'll teach you to leave Monsieur Dimanche to kick his heels in an antechamber! You shall learn a little more discrimination.

M. DIMANCHE: Please say no more about it, Sir.

DON JUAN: [*to* M. DIMANCHE] What! Deny me to you; to Monsieur Dimanche, my best friend?

M. DIMANCHE: Monsieur, I am your most devoted servant. I came to ...

DON JUAN: A seat there for Monsieur Dimanche!

M. DIMANCHE: I shall do very well as I am, Sir.

DON JUAN: By no means. I want you to come here and sit by me.

M. DIMANCHE: It's really not necessary, Sir.

DON JUAN: Take this stool away, and bring an armchair.

M. DIMANCHE: You can't be serious, Sir. I ...

DON JUAN: No, no, I know what's due to you. I wish there to be no distinction between us.

M. DIMANCHE: Sir ...

DON JUAN: Come, sit down.

M. DIMANCHE: There's no occasion at all, Sir. I have very little to say. I was ...

DON JUAN: Sit down, I beg of you.

M. DIMANCHE: No, Sir. I am quite alright. I came to ...

DON JUAN: I won't listen, unless you sit down.

M. DIMANCHE: Very well then, Sir; if you wish it. I ...

DON JUAN: I hope I see you well, Monsieur Dimanche.

M. DIMANCHE: Oh, yes, Sir, thank you kindly. I have come to ...

DON JUAN: You have a regular fund of good health; full lips, fresh colour, and bright eyes.

M. DIMANCHE: I would ...

DON JUAN: How is Madame Dimanche, your wife?

M. DIMANCHE: In good health, Sir, I thank God.

DON JUAN: A splendid woman!

M. DIMANCHE: She is your humble servant, Sir. I came ...

DON JUAN: And Claudine, your little girl? How is she?

M. DIMANCHE: Quite well.[29] [End of excerpt]

MS: There is also the celebrated autumn scene in the forest with the beggar.

[Excerpt of Act 3, scene 2]

DON JUAN: How do you pass your time here among all these trees?

MAN: I pray all day long for the prosperity of the kind people who give me alms.

DON JUAN: You are quite comfortably off then, I suppose?

MAN: Alas, no Sir! I am in the greatest penury.

DON JUAN: What? A man who prays all day long can't fail to be well off.

MAN: I assure you, Sir, I often haven't even a crust to put in my mouth.

DON JUAN: That's strange. You're not very well rewarded for your trouble. See here. I'll give you a gold Louis, if you'll utter a blasphemy.

MAN: Oh, Sir, would you have me commit such a terrible sin?

DON JUAN: The question is, do you want this gold piece or not? I'll give it to you if you blaspheme. Come now.

MAN: Sir ...

DON JUAN: You shan't have it unless you do.

SGANARELLE: Come along! Just one little blasphemy. There's no harm in it.

DON JUAN: Here you are; take it! Take it, I say. Blaspheme.

MAN: No, Sir. I would rather die of starvation.

DON JUAN: Oh very well then. I give it you for the love of ... humanity.[30] [End of excerpt]

MS: We can easily see that in the scene with Mr Dimanche, Dom Juan does not pay him with money but entertains him with words. In the scene with the beggar, he gives him money but, as he says, for the "love of humanity" and in exchange for a word, that is, for a testimony, or rather, a blaspheme. In the end, with the wages for his valet, it is shown that he, Sganarelle, has not been paid and, as such, Dom Juan's behavior vis-à-vis money is a refusal of the law of gift exchange that tobacco is a model of. With respect to the question of words, that is to say, vis-à-vis of oath-taking, Dom Juan will have the same behavior of breaking with the law of gift exchange. For that which concerns women, it is the same. I will not develop this much further but I would simply say that there is a model of disobedience of the hero vis-à-vis words, vis-à-vis money, and vis-à-vis women. The law of gift exchange is seized on the level of tobacco and is its reduced model.

AB: In this case, I think we could speak of a structuralist critique. This permits us to define structure and structural critique when structure is not a principle of organization for the totality of the work but an organizing mould of which a model would be figured in the interior of the work. It is in the successive reiteration of the model that we find the very principle for an elucidation of the work.

MS: We can say that the demonstration recommences with respect to each model.

AB: Might we conclude with some precepts from all this?

MS: I believe that we might say something to the audience, in particular to the high school seniors. What I would say is something on the order of ethics or suspicion. First, when you speak of structure, it is necessary to be cautious of all the devalued senses that it can take. That is to say, when you speak of structure, it should be clear that one is not necessarily raising a structure when one has merely raised an organization or arrangement. Secondly, having said a lot on this, when it concerns a model, there is also a precept of suspicion because the method of using models is a method by analogy or simulation and if there is a notion where caution should be undertaken, it's the notion of analogy. Thus, we have the suspicion of architecture and suspicion of analogies.

AB: Finally, in what concerns the pair "structure and model," I believe that it is important not to be too tied up with the pair "abstract and concrete" because our whole effort has been to demonstrate that the relation between structure and model operates with a much more detailed kind of stratification, epistemologically speaking, than the classic pair "abstract and concrete."

Notes

1   This transcription and translation can only take account of the second and third parts of the interview. The first part of the series is, despite our extensive search, lost in a forgotten basement. Thanks goes to François Farellacci for help with the French transcription. A reference to this interview was given by Badiou in his *Le Concept de Modèle*. Alain Badiou, *Le Concept de Modèle* (Paris: Maspero, 1969), 91. Unlike the other interviews collected in this volume, this interview contains a series of montages which are briefly described in brackets, including a bibliographic reference for a reading from an excerpt of Claude Levi-Strauss' *Structural Anthropology*. However, the longer

montages taken from the film adaptation of Molière's *Dom Juan* in 1965 by the director Marcel Blüwal are cited in the text itself from an English translation by Ian Maclean and published by Oxford University Press. Since the content of the text is necessary for the understanding of the interview, remaining with a mere bibliographic reference would undermine the readability of the transcript.

2 Badiou alludes here to Lévi-Strauss and to others who followed in his attempt of importing formalization in the human sciences.

3 A few months before the recording of this dialogue, Serres had published an important article on "Analyse symbolique et méthode structurale." Michel Serres, "Analyse symbolique et méthode structurale," *Revue philosophique de la France et de l'Etranger*, 4 (1967): 437–52.

4 The term "metaxu" or μεταξύis [or methexis, μεθεξις] is the Greek term for "between" or "intermediate." It arises canonically in discussions of Plato's theory of forms, how things in flux "participate" in immutable forms. A typical reference to this concept in Plato can be found in the book five of the *Republic* at 477a5: "Now, if anything is such as to be and also not to be, won't it be intermediate between what purely is and what in no way is? Yes, it's intermediate." Plato, *Complete Works*, ed. by John M. Cooper, trans. by G. M. A. Grube and C. D. C. Reeve (Indianapolis and Cambridge: Hackett Publishing Company, 1997), 1103.

5 It seems that Serres is making reference to his own book on Leibniz, *Le système de Leibniz et ses modèles mathématiques* published in 1968. In it he refers, on the question of a model's *"fidélité,"* to Leibniz's short essay, "What is an idea?", where the latter takes up the difference between an idea and a thought as well as describes his theory of expression. In the context of the interview, it is worth noting that Leibniz argues that ideas have the particular function of expression, where a thing expresses certain relations present in another. Leibniz argues that, by a function of similitude, a smaller circle can express the relations of a larger one and a circle can express the optical or perspectival expression of an ellipse. Ultimately, Leibniz's point is that the world represents god in some sense just as the actions of an individual represents their soul. In Serres' text, he highlights the essay as the development of one sense of "model" that is at work in Leibniz's thought. Michel Serres, *Le système de Leibniz et ses modèles mathématiques*, 4th edn (Paris: PUF, 2007), 57. Cf. G. W. Leibniz, "What is an idea?" in *Philosophical Papers and Letters*, 2nd edn, trans. and ed. by Leroy Loemker (Dordrecht: Kluwer Academic Publishers, 1989), 207–8.

6   *L'Inondation* (*The Flood*) is an 1880 novella by Émile Zola. Set in the village of Saint-Jory, several miles up the Garonne from Toulouse, it is the story of a family tragedy, told by its patriarch, seventy-year-old Louis Roubien.

7   Tesserae are small cubes, made of wood, bone, ivory and the like, used in Roman antiquity as a ticket, tally, or token. In a different sense, the pieces that compose a mosaic are also tesserae.

8   The discoveries in genetics by James D. Watson and Francis Crick put back biology in the center of attention. But it is especially in 1965 with François Jacob, André Lwoff, and Jacques Monod's Nobel prize that the life sciences become very important in the French philosophical field. Those discoveries would serve to encourage the reflection of formalization by Lévi-Strauss, Canguilhem, and Hyppolite.

9   A major critical point of the interview, on the uses and abuses of models in the history and practice of science and literature might be said to be a uniting theme of Gaston Bachelard's diverse *oeuvre*. The debate surrounding waves and particles in modern physics is the main theme in Gaston Bachelard's *Le nouvel esprit scientifique*, first published in 1934. In it, Bachelard proposes a "Non" or "Anti-Cartesian" epistemology that would attempt to synthesize the dialectical fault lines of contemporary physics. This includes a critique of notions of substance, atomism, and reductionism explicit or at times latent in contemporary science. Another long discussion of the history of the development of atomic structure is undertaken by Bachelard in *Le rationalisme appliqué*, published in 1949. The notion of the model as an "obstacle" is the major theme of Bachelard's *La Formation de l'esprit scientifique*, published in 1938, which highlights common sense, unity, substance, realism, the animal, and digestion as forms of "obstacles" in the development of science and rationality. Gaston Bachelard, *Le nouvel esprit scientifique*, 7th edn (Paris: PUF, 2003). Gaston Bachelard, *Le rationalism appliqué*, 4th edn (Paris: PUF, 2004). Gaston Bachelard, *La Formation de l'esprit scientifique*, 6th edn (Paris: Vrin, 1969).

10 In this context, I have translated Serres' use of "*adjuvant*" by "catalyst." This term occurs a few more times in the text. The French term refers to a substance that has a positive or ameliorative effect. In the context of scientific inquiry, it seems that "catalyst" is the most appropriate in English despite the literal reference to catalysts in the previous discussion of unidirectional relations.

11 Cristallography has been an topic of interest for French empistemology since Hélène Metzger's 1918 *La genèse de la science*

des cristaux. Cf. Hélène Metzger, *La genèse de la science des cristaux* (Paris: PUF, 1969).

12 At this time, Serres had just published an essay on graphs. Michel Serres, "Pénélope ou d'un graphe théorique,"*Revue philosophique*, 1 (1966): 41–51.

13 Bachelard speaks incessantly of epistemological obstacles and uses the movement away from Bohr's atom to express this. Cf. Gaston Bachelard, *Le matérialisme rationnel* (Paris: PUF, 1953), 215–17.

14 A "trial balloon" is often used in the context of a media proposition meant to test a public's impression or opinion to a proposition or action. This seems to be what Serres means by the term insofar as the expression concerns counter-examples "popping," as it were, certain balloons. The expression has its roots in the launching of balloon to recuperate meteorological data, a sense which might be closer to the French usage. In any case, Serres makes it quite clear what he means by the term.

15 See note 8.

16 This will be the point of departure on Serres' reflection in his project *Hermes*. Cf. Michel Serres, *Hermes: Literature, Science and Philosophy*, trans. and ed. by Josué V. Harari and David F. Bell (Baltimore: Johns Hopkins University Press, 1982).

17 Badiou is here referring to the work of the Society for the Study of Poetic Language founded in 1916 in St Petersburg (then Petrograd) by Boris Eichenbaum, Viktor Shklovsky, and Yury Tynyanov, and secondarily to the Moscow Linguistic Circle founded in 1914 by Roman Jakobson. It was especially Vladimir Propp, often associated with the movement, who studied folklore.

18 Claude Lévi-Strauss, *Anthropologie structurale* (Paris: Librarie Plon, 1974), 244.

19 This phrase appears in Lacan's *Seminar XX* where he speaks precisely on the status of the "as" in the context of psychoanalytical discourse. The distinction between being structured "like" and being structured "by" is clearly at work. "You see that by still preserving this 'like' (*comme*), I am staying within the bounds of what I put forward when I say that the unconscious is structured like a language. I say *like* so as not to say ... that the unconscious is structured *by* a language." Jacques Lacan, *Seminar XX: Encore, On Feminine Sexuality and the Limits of Love and Knowledge 1972–1973*, trans. by Bruce Fink (New York and London, W. W. Norton and Company, 1998), 48.

20 See note 12 of "Philosophy and Science" in this volume, *infra*.

21 This refers to part one of the filmed interviews which would have

been entitled "*Modèle et structure: partie I, Philosophie n° 40.*"
While Badiou and Serres make reference to this first part of their
conversation here, the lack does not seem to render the section of
conversation incomprehensible.

22 Henri Michaux was a poet, writer, and painter connected
to the surrealist movement who wrote, among other works,
autobiographical and imaginary travel journals. It is likely that Badiou
is here refering to texts like *Ailleurs* of 1948, which is a collection
of imaginary travel journals describing fictional peoples, fauna, and
flora. Henri Michaux, *Ailleurs* (Paris, Gallimard, 1986).

23 Michel Serres treats these questions in his "Don Juan au palais des
merveilles: Sur les statues au XVIIe siècle." Cf. Michel Serres, "Don
Juan au palais des merveilles: Sur les statues au XVIIe siècle," *Les
Etudes philosophiques*, 3 (1966): 385–90. Serres then published a
longer version of this reflection in the first volume of his *Hermes*
under the title of "The Apparition of Hermes: *Dom Juan*." Cf. Michel
Serres, "The Apparition of Hermes: *Dom Juan*," in *Hermes*, 3–14.

24 *Essai sur le don* is translated and published as *The Gift: The Form
and Reason of Exchange in Archaic Societies*. Cf. Marcel Mauss, *The
Gift: The Form and Reason of Exchange in Archaic Societies* (New
York and London, W. W. Norton and Company, 2000).

25 The praise of tobacco occurs in the opening lines of *Dom Juan*.
Rather than translating Molière from the interview, this sentence
and the following passages are taken from George Graveley and Ian
Maclean's English translation. Molière, *Don Juan and other plays*, ed.
by Ian Maclean, trans. by George Graveley and Ian Maclean (Oxford,
Oxford University Press, 1998), 33.

26 Marcel Blüwal's *Dom Juan ou le festin de pierre* was made in 1965
in black and white and intended for television. Don Juan was played
by Michel Piccoli, his faithful valet Sganarelle was played by Claude
Brasseur and Dona Elvira, the Don's wife, was played by Anouk
Ferjac.

27 Molière, *Don Juan*, 33.

28 Molière, *Don Juan*, 91.

29 Molière, *Don Juan*, 72–5.

30 Molière, *Don Juan*, 63–4.

CHAPTER NINE

Teaching philosophy through television

Dina Dreyfus with excerpts from the broadcasts of 1965 by Jean Hyppolite, Georges Canguilhem, Raymond Aron, Michel Foucault, Paul Ricoeur, and, by telephone, Alain Badiou

First broadcast: 4 June 1965

Dina Dreyfus: I thank all the teachers who are here today for listening to me and I hope to excuse myself from the very meager dessert that this episode represents in view of the substantial meal, philosophically speaking, that the six other episodes represented. Today, I propose a synthesis and yet it is not a complete synthesis. In fact, I received, and I warmly thank the teachers, many reports, lists of questions, letters, the conversations that they initiated with me. We had a day of synthesis in Rennes and in all this, we need to make a collection of all of this. This collecting together constitutes a considerable volume and a report that corresponds to all the responses that I received and I believe that, I hope that, it will be widely broadcasted by the administrators of the educational television and will in any case be published in a future volume of the *Revue de l'enseignement philosophique*.

Thus today, I will evoke for you some of the essential questions and which constitutes the focus of the objections, the suggestions, the wishes, in any case, the remarks [that I received]. The first of these questions is the choice of subjects and the choice of the order of the subjects. I had the occasion to allude to this choice and this order in a short article for the *Bulletin de la television scolaire*[1] and in which I said that this choice and this order was deliberate. That is to say that the exclusions that were made may have been surprising but were the result of a wish for unity, given the time limits that were afforded to us, and signifies that certain absolutely important and even essential questions like those of the relation of philosophy and ethics would find their place in the episodes that will follow. At this time, this year, I have simply proposed to compare philosophy with what is not philosophical, in thinking through the sort of confrontation that allows us to elucidate the function of philosophy against what is not [philosophical]. This is what I believe to be the meaning of the response that Mr Canguilhem gave to Badiou in the second episode.

[Excerpt from "Philosophy and science"][2]

Alain Badiou: There is however a level of meaning where science needs philosophy

Georges Canguilhem: No doubt there exists a level of meaning where science needs philosophy because science does not contain in itself the question of its own meaning. The response to the question of the meaning of science is something that is – I won't say furnished – by philosophy, but is what it is supposed to furnish. [End of excerpt]

DD: This is also the meaning of Mr Aron's affirmation.

[Excerpt from "Philosophy and sociology"]

Raymond Aron: All the philosophers of the Western tradition are, in one way or another, moralists and all or almost all attached their reflections on human existence and morality to a certain explicit or implicit representation of society. And there is, it seems to me, a danger in how a moralist loses track of the social reality of her times or with the transformation of this social reality, especially in times of rapid upheaval like today. I do not want to say at all that ultimate moral values or the ultimate moral reflection depends on the structure of society, I don't know. At least this is the philosophical question on which I cannot come to a decision. But I think that we might renew certain classical themes of moral philosophy by placing this theme in relation to the proper problems of social order today. [End of excerpt]

DD: ... to the response to Mr Foucault.

[Excerpt from "Philosophy and psychology"]

Michel Foucault: [I]n being the most universal cultural form, something happened in philosophy, the means by which the West has reflected on itself, at a certain moment in time in this cultural form and the reflection that it permits. Something fundamental happened at the beginning of the nineteenth century or maybe already at the end of the eighteenth century. This event was the appearance of what we might call reflection in the anthropological style. That is to say, what appeared at this moment, for the first time, is an inquiry that Kant formulated in his *Logic*, "What is man?" [End of excerpt]

DD: Concerning the first episode, it should be considered an opening, an introduction, since regardless of the form of teaching, we should always ask ourselves what is pregiven and what relation philosophy has with history. It is to this question that Mr Hyppolite gave his response.

[Excerpt from "Philosophy and its history"]

Jean Hyppolite: Well, I think we can't, at least not today, philosophize without the history of philosophy, that is, the history of the great philosophical works and the great systems of the past. When you want to initiate someone into philosophy, since you are a philosophy teacher as I am, you need to put them in contact with the philosophers of the past. This is exactly as if one wanted to learn poetry, there is only one way: read the poets. [End of excerpt]

DD: And the fifth episode could be considered a conclusion to the idea that philosophy is a language and to teach philosophy is thus to use language in a double sense. This is the sense of the first sentences of Mr Ricoeur in his episode.

[Excerpt from "Philosophy and language"]

Paul Ricoeur: [P]hilosophy has always been a struggle for clarity, for clarification, and for coherence. And in this aim its work is a linguistic work of a particular and privileged form. It is in reflection and in philosophical speculation that all the problems of signs and meanings from other disciplines are contemplated. [End of excerpt]

DD: The second question is that of the depth of the interviews. Many found these interviews to be quite difficult: philosophy is difficult. And television, if it is aimed at making accessible what could not be so without it, is not aimed at making it easier. In any case, here as elsewhere, the professor remains the mediator between philosophy, regardless of its form of expression, and the students. But above all, I want to insist on the fact that the difficulties to which I made allusion are not difficulties in terms of vocabulary. First because the technical vocabulary is not an insurmountable difficulty to the degree that technical terms are the most easy to explain and for which there is always a possible definition. But on the other hand, I want to remind us that these technical terms are defined in accompanying texts. On the other hand, during the course of these very episodes, certain technical terms have been explained or defined by the professors themselves. As such Aron consecrated a part of his discussion to define the term ideology.

[Excerpt from "Philosophy and sociology"]

Raymond Aron: One of my colleagues who has a taste for distinctions has found 13 meanings for the word "ideology." I will save you this great number of these meanings. We can simply say that I see at least three principal ones.

First of all, regardless of which political party or individual, if one tries to synthesize one's attitude with regard to reality or one's vision of reality, we turn these abstract ideas into something that we would call "ideology." This is to say, we get a stark presentation capable of convincing someone else of one's representation of the political world or objectives. In this sense, any political party possesses a certain degree of ideology, even the most conservative ones or the least ideological ones.

There is a second meaning, the meaning that arises when we can speak of a Marxist ideology or, with a bit more difficulty, of a fascist ideology. I call this the systematic formation of what any political party possesses, that is to say, a group of ideas. And the systematization, the representation of the historical past and the future of a group, provides an ideological system, something that is at the same time much stronger and much more rigorous but also more false in the sense of ideology in the weak sense that I spoke about a moment ago.

And then there is a third sense that interests me the most. This is what we find in Marx. This is ideology as false representation or a justificatory representation of the world. Starting from this point, you have a problem that is at the same time sociological and philosophical. That is, what is it to be someone in relation to the idea created by oneself? What is it to be a class or a society with respect to the idea that this class or this society created of itself? [End of excerpt]

DD: Foucault defined the expression "cultural form."

[Excerpt from "Philosophy and psychology"]

MF: Well, by "cultural form" I understand, if you like, the manner in which cultural data such as an organized or institutionalized knowledge frees up a language that is proper to it and eventually reaches a form that one could call "scientific" or "para-scientific." [End of excerpt]

DD: Ricoeur gave the definition of "semantics."

[Excerpt from "Philosophy and language"]

PR: If we generally define semantics as a domain of meaningful unities ... [End of excerpt]

DD: Of "polysemy."

[Excerpt from "Philosophy and language"]

PR: And we encounter the problem of the multiplicity of meanings, that of polysemy ... [End of excerpt]

DD: Of "hermeneutics" and "exegesis."

[Excerpt from "Philosophy and language"]

PR: We might distinguish hermeneutics and exegesis in the following way. Exegesis is the interpretation of a text and hermeneutics is a reflection on the rules of reading that orders the exegesis of a determined text. [End of excerpt]

DD: The question of the depth of the interviews has in any case given place to another objection, or rather given rise to same objection, since the difficulty of the interviews resulted in the problem that the teacher had to dedicate a lot of time in explanation and in preparing students. Here I believe that there is perhaps, here also, a certain misunderstanding. It seems to me that we need to find norms for the [use] of television broadcasts and how it presides in the lesson, in the explication of texts which are the forms of expression which have their own proper norms or in a broadcasted radio broadcast.

For if we want these texts to be accompanied by the image, in television broadcasts, an explication of texts, we thus not only in effect need a very considerable amount of time for explanation and in preparation but also we fall upon another inconvenience that is very serious in my opinion. We disassociate the image from sound and we make sound an autonomous and self-sufficient element when we convert it into a text of explanation and, as such, forget the image. In this we bring up the question that I will examine further, that is, the relation of speech and image.

In any case, in the episodes of this year, without giving a complete explication of text, which, in effect, I repeat, would have demanded a considerable amount of time, it seems to me that it was possible to find some powerful moments, I would say essential moments. I prefer to call them powerful moments because this better shows the strict collaboration between image and speech. If we look for them, it seems very clear to me that we can distinguish powerful moments from essential moments. They are powerful from the point of view of impression and essential from the point of view of signification. These powerful moments are, in all the episodes, those in which we ultimately question the nature of philosophy, of the definition of philosophy.

[Excerpt from "Philosophy and its history"]

JH: [T]he philosophical systems of the past represent a first degree of thinking, if I dare say. This is not thinking itself but gives us a sort of existent metaphysical thinking with this double character and this double character is the link between a matter and a form. I mean the thought of a philosopher is a thought that wants to think being, that wants to think content, unlike mathematical thought, for example, and it is at the same time a thinking that wants to be rigorous and not arbitrary. For them, the knowledge of knowledge and the knowledge of being are coupled together. [End of excerpt]

DD: We also find this with Mr Foucault.

[Excerpt from "Philosophy and psychology"]

MF: [P]hilosophy is probably the most characteristic and the most general cultural form in the Western world. Since the beginning of Greek thought until Heidegger, until now, philosophy has been the means through which Western culture has perpetually continued to reflect on itself. In this sense, philosophy is not a cultural form but is the most general cultural form of our culture. [End of excerpt]

DD: But above all we find all this in the sixth episode, since – and there is nothing surprising about this – the sixth episode was completely dedicated to the problem of the relation between scientific truth and philosophical truth with respect to the problem that is ultimately a perpetual one, the nature of philosophy. We found ourselves before a certain number of conceptions of philosophy, none of which were affronted but were, at least, confronted. We saw this in a number of times where Mr Ricoeur formulated his own conception.

[Excerpt from "Philosophy and truth"]

PR: [P]hilosophy should be considered as a space of confrontation between, on the one hand, the formal task of coherence and on the other hand, the effort to get a hold on what is ultimately in question for philosophy, that is, through this multiplicity of meaning, what is. [...] [W]e are interested in philosophy because each one constitutes an internal relation, in short, between its questions and its answers and in so doing determining the field, in short, of its own truth. It interests us because we have the conviction or the hope that through these finite works the human mind produces an encounter with the same being ... [End of excerpt]

DD: And then that of Badiou.

[Excerpt from "Philosophy and truth"]

Alain Badiou: Would you accept us saying that a philosophy is something that is a center of the totalization of the experience of an epoch which is extended across the ambiguity of relations that brings itself to operate within the framework of a code or a language which on the one hand imports the criteria of rigor, or even coherence, of science. [End of excerpt]

DD: Badiou was affirmed by Canguilhem and Hyppolite who drew from norms for judging what is a great philosophy and from determining the meaning of a "great philosophy." What is a great philosophy?

[Excerpt from "Philosophy and truth"]

GC: If it is true that philosophy should be popularized in a non-vulgar way, as Hyppolite said, this popularization of different codes adopted by the science in their path of constitution, through all the cultural activities of a given epoch, it seems to me that there is a fundamentally naïve side, I would even say a popular side, of philosophy that we tend too often to neglect and perhaps a great philosophy is a philosophy that left behind an adjective in popular language. Plato gave us something "platonic," the stoics delivered something "stoic," Descartes delivered something "Cartesian," Kant something "Kantian" as well as an "categorical imperative." In other words, there are philosophers who, because they totalized the experience of an epoch and succeeded in disseminating themselves outside of the philosophical but in the modes of culture which would themselves be totalized by another philosophy and have in this sense a direct impact on what we could call our common experience, in our daily lives, our quotidian experience.

[...]

JH: In such a way a great philosophy is a philosophy that is capable of being translated in a certain way into the common language of all. Simply put, we should also distinguish totalization which we are all in agreement on and a totalization, in order to have a point of impact which is often a partial totalization and through the point of impact something almost partial. In this way the sharp character of philosophical genius – for we find something here, something that touches genius – comes into contact with its own epoch, not through the work of their inheritors, that is to say, not in what is accumulated, but rather in a deep contact with what the epoch pronounces in a stammer.

GC: Certainly. [End of excerpt]

DD: And finally the conception of Hyppolite that complies with that of Canguilhem, Ricoeur, and Badiou.

[Excerpt from "Philosophy and truth"]

JH: A sense of totality only remains in philosophy and we could not at all evacuate this from our vision.

GC: No, this is the very definition of philosophy.

JH: The more sciences become cultural and less cosmic, less totalizing, the more it will need a philosophy to unite human beings. Philosophy will be that much more indispensable while science gets closer to truth, rigorous and technical truth, the truth of a special domain. The more it will need a return to this essence of philosophy.

GC: Absolutely agree.

[...]

JH: Could I simply intervene here in saying that you said that there is neither object nor nature, nor cosmos, nor universe, for science. At the present moment, the sciences, in their extremely specialized aspects, establish their truth entirely. To this degree we reserve this totality for ourselves. In this we are caught up, we are held in *this* totality: nature, cosmos, human beings.

GC: I have said nothing else.

[...]

JH: [I]t is no longer possible today to have a philosophical thought that resembles that of ancient ontology, that is to say, to a pre-given theory? Hence since there is no longer theology there is then also no longer any pre-existing objective categories for science ...

GC: There is no theology, there are no pre-existing objective categories for science. And so I am not surprised to see that among the auditors there might be those who are surprised ... you said, my dear Badiou, that I caused a scandal. I do not believe that I could scandalize you. I am even certain that I will not scandalize you, but you are among those who were surprised by the proposition that I aimed toward. There are those for whom philosophy is ultimately a substitute for theology or those who think that they now have the means to transform philosophy into science.

JH: ... into objective categories that substitute an active revolutionary thought. [End of excerpt]

DD: He also made some objections to the very form of the interview, not the interview but the form that it took during the course of the episode. Some have questioned Mr Badiou on having taken the course of a dialogue of traps and of disingenuous turns. What did we know? Some reproached him of passivity. Finally, some reproached him of not submitting to a Socratic model. And Mr Badiou himself responded to this objection.

AB: [voice off, by telephone] We have compared in sum the episodes with the implicit model of the Socratic dialogue. Here we should not in any case forget one point: this is that we are very exactly in an inverse situation. For in a Socratic dialogue the one who questions is the master. In a television broadcast, it is not for a second in question for me that I could be considered the master of Hyppolite, of Canguilhem or of Ricoeur. When I interrogate them I am in no way in the situation of a Socratic dialogue. We should [instead] understand that it is a situation where I am the one who is interrogated. The function of my questions cannot clearly be other that the mediation of their respective speech. What we have advanced is the image of a punctuated monologue. I would rather say that I accept the idea of a mediated rather than punctuated speech and this mediation of their own speech through the questions and difficulties through which I could from time to time confront. This was simply my ambition and it was thus limited.

DD: For this we only need to hear certain responses of Alain Badiou to give an account of what was actually a mediated speech, as he has said himself, in opposition to what we call a punctuated speech.

[Montage of Alain Badiou's interview style and use of expressions like "but then," "even so," "should we understand by what you say then that ..." etc.]

DD: The last and most important question for me, since it engages with the enterprise itself, is the question that could be brutally formulated in the following way: why television? This question asks why we did not do something through radio. With respect to the scope of the question I might simply answer in saying that you should listen and watch and decide for yourselves.

[Excerpt from "Philosophy and psychology"]

AB: You have distinguished two perspectives. In the first, philosophy in sum opens up the domain of psychology but the human sciences take it up in an effective and positive way. In the second perspective which we have underlined as your preference, anthropology is entirely taken up as an end point in philosophy as the cultural form through which the West has come to think of itself or attempts to achieve self-reflection. So, if you like, I would like to ask my question again relative to the essence of psychology at both of these levels. First, if we admit that philosophy had totally and implicitly prescribed its domain to the human sciences in general, where human sciences would be the storehouse of old philosophical questions, in this perspective, by admitting that you could provisionally mime it, what gives the specificity of psychology in the context of these other projects that we designate communally as the "human sciences?" [End of excerpt]

DD: I could also respond by saying that no one exists only as a voice, As Mr Canguilhem puts it more profoundly, it is perhaps possible that the human face can only be perceived as an image such that we cannot say that the televised image approaches or distances us from reality. But regardless of the quality, the close relation between its quality and life is not only different from spoken discourse without image but it is also different from life.

This means, or better, this shows that I did not want to interpret what we just showed as a contestation of the absolute autonomy of language of its supremacy, not only in the teaching of philosophy, that goes without saying, but also not in teaching in general, this also goes without saying, but in human relations, whatever they are. I mean that language is and remains the milieu that brings about the most specific human relations and this clarifies what I did not mean to say. I only wanted to say the following, that I wanted to accomplish something, if we really want that there is not only a speech that is accompanied by an image and above all a documentary image, which I am suspicious of, we need to look, we need to find a way of placing an inseparable totality in which speech and image appear together with all the complementary images and not, as I have said, to believe in a language of images. I actually believe that this expression is a bit dangerous. But without believing in a language of images we can believe that the image has meaning if not a signification and since language is the maker and giver of meaning, it can also be given into the image which is ready to receive it.

Notes

1 Dina Dreyfus, 'L'enseignement de la philosophie et la télévision: Synthèse des émission de l'année 1964–1965,' *Dossiers pédagogiques de la radio-télévision scolaire* 17 (1965): 49–52.

2 This except is taken from an edit of "Philosophy and Science" that is not included in the version in this volume. Canguilhem says something very similar but this excerpt is not reproduced here. See infra.

APPENDIX A

Short biographies of participants

This series of short biographies is meant to provide a context for the lives of the participants when they entered into these interviews from 1965 to 1968. The list is ordered chronologically according to year of birth.

GEORGES CANGUILHEM

Born in 1904 in Castelnaudary (France), Canguilhem entered the *Ecole Normale Supérieure* in 1924 (the same year as Jean-Paul Sartre, Raymond Aron, Daniel Lagache, Raymond Badiou, etc.). A faithful pupil of the Kantian philosopher and secondary school teacher Alain, after his *agrégation* in 1927, he started teaching in different secondary schools in the south of France and writing short political essays for the journal *Les Libres Propos* and *Europe* (now gathered in the first tome of his *Œuvres completes*). In 1935, animated by the two philosophical problems of norms and of the relation between science and technique, Canguilhem started studying medicine and in 1943 and he accomplished his doctoral dissertation, *The Normal and the Pathological*. Starting from 1941, he began teaching philosophy at the University of Strasbourg, taking over the chair from his friend Jean Cavaillès. In 1943–4 he engaged in the *Résistance* in the Auvergne region. In 1949 he became president of the commission, *l'Inspection générale de philosophie*, charged with evaluating secondary school philosophy education. In 1955, after the defense of his two Ph.D. dissertations (*La connaissance de la vie* and *La formation du concept de réflexe aux XVII et XVIII siècles*) he succeeded Gaston Bachelard as the director of the Sorbonne *Institut d'histoire des sciences*. From 1964 until 1968 he served as the president of the jury of the *agrégation*. In 1968 he published some of his studies in *Etudes d'histoire et de philosophie des sciences*.

RAYMOND ARON

Born in 1905 in Paris, he attended Condorcet secondary school and entered the *École normale supérieure* in 1924 where he obtained his *agrégation* in 1929. From 1930 until 1933 he studied in Germany (Cologne and Berlin) where he witnessed the rise of the Nazi regime. He taught one year at Le Havre secondary school and then become secretary of the *Centre de documentation sociale* of the *École normale supérieure* and professor of the *École normale supérieure d'enseignement primaire* in Paris. After having defended his two doctoral dissertations in 1938 (*Introduction to the Philosophy of History* and *Essay on the theory of history in contemporary Germany*) he was appointed professor of social philosophy in University of Toulouse. After the defeat of France he fled to London where he became editor of the journal *La France Libre* (the essays he wrote in the journal will later be published in the book *Chroniques de guerre*). At the *Libération* he came back to Paris and created, with Jean-Paul Sartre, Merelau-Ponty and Simone de Beauvoir, the journal *Les Temps Modernes* that he would eventually leave in 1947 to join the editorial board of the *Figaro*. From 1945 to 1947 he taught in Paris at *École nationale d'administration* and from 1948 to 1954 at the *Institut d'études politique*. In 1955, just after the publication of his best-seller *The Opium of the Intellectuals* he become lecturer and, from 1958, professor of sociology at the *Sorbonne*. The following year Aron was responsible for the creation of a *"licence"* [Bachelor's degree] in sociology and he created the *Centre de sociologie européenne*. Among the dozen of books that Aron published during the 60s were: *Dimensions de la conscience historique* (1961), *La Lutte des classes* (1964), *Démocratie et totalitarisme* (1965) and *Les Étapes de la pensée sociologique* (1967).

JEAN HYPPOLITE

Born in Jonzac on 8 January 1907, Hyppolite entered the *Ecole Normale* in 1927 and befriended Jean-Paul Sartre and Maurice Merleau-Ponty. He obtained his *agrégation* in 1931. During the 30s he taught at various secondary schools and during the early 40s in the prestigious *Henri IV* secondary school. In 1947 he obtained his doctorate with the translation of Hegel's *Phenomenology of Spirit* (published in two volumes, 1939 and 1941) and with a book of commentary *The Genesis and Structure of the Phenomenology of Spirit*. From 1946 until 1949 he taught at the University of Strasbourg and, from 1949 on, at the Sorbonne. During the 50s he became interested in "late" Heidegger and in Marx's "early" thought. In 1952 he published a very influential book on Hegel's logic, *Logique et existence*. In 1954, he became the director of the *Ecole Normale Supérieure*. In 1963 he was elected to the "Histoire de la pensée philosophique" chair at the *Collège de France* where he taught seminars on Hegel and on the relation between "sense and time" starting from perspectives as diverse as information theory, Bergsonism, Hegelianism, and phenomenology. He supervised many of the projects of Michel Foucault, Michel Henry, Gilles Deleuze, Jacques Derrida, Alain Badiou and others. His book series, "Epimethée," through the *Presses Universitaries Françaises*, which continues today, was a central reference throughout the 50s and 60s.

DINA DREYFUS

Born in Milan on 1 February 1911 to a Jewish family of Russian origin, Dreyfus arrived in France in 1924 studying philosophy and anthropology at the Sorbonne and obtaining the *agrégation* in 1933. Between 1935 and 1938 she participated, with her then husband Claude Lévi-Strauss, in the French cultural mission at the University of São Paulo. She gave a series of lectures on practical anthropology and founded, with Mário de Andrade, the first Brazilian ethnological society and participated, with Lévi-Strauss and Luiz de Castro Faria, in a series of studies on the Bororos and Nambikwara tribes that resulted in an exposition in Paris (*Indiens du Mato-Grosso. Mission Claude et Dina Lévi-Strauss*, catalogue, 1937). During the German occupation she joined the *Résistance* in the region of Montpellier. After the war she taught in several high schools and she became *l'Inspectrice générale de philosophie* and developed an interest in the relation between philosophy, pedagogy, and visual mediums. During the 50s she published a number of articles in the reviews *Mercure de France*, *Diogène*, and *Les Temps modernes* and edited a collection of texts by Freud entitled *Psychanalyse* in 1967.

PAUL RICŒUR

Born on 27 February 1913 in Valence to a protestant family, Ricœur received his undergraduate degree from the Sorbonne in 1934 and in 1935 passed the *agrégation*. During the 30s he participated in several journals of the Christian left wing. Mobilized during the war, he was captured by the Germans and spent five years as a prisoner of war, during which he began translating Husserl's *Ideen* and reading Karl Jaspers, on which he would publish a book in 1948 (*Philosophie du mystère et philosophie du paradoxe*). Between 1948 and 1956 he taught at the University of Strasbourg and in 1950 defended his two Ph.D. dissertations, the translation of *Ideen I* and *Freedom and Nature: The Voluntary and the Involuntary*. In 1955 he collected some of his philosophical and political essays in the book *History and Truth*. In 1956 he began teaching at the Sorbonne. While at the Sorbonne, he wrote three works: *Fallible Man: The Voluntary and the Involuntary II*, *The Symbolism of Evil* (both published in 1960) and *Freud and Philosophy: An Essay on Interpretation* published in 1965. Based in a hermeneutical perspective, at the beginning of the 60s he turned toward the problem of language, discussing the work of Lévi-Strauss, in the group around the *Esprit* journal. In 1965 he began teaching at the University of Paris Nanterre.

MICHEL HENRY

Born on 10 January 1922 in Haiphong (Viêt Nam), Michel Henry studied at the prestigious *Henri IV* secondary school under the supervision of Jean Guéhenno. He entered the *Ecole Normale Supérieure* in 1940. In 1943, under the supervision of Jean Grenier, he wrote his DES [*diplôme d'études supérieures*] dissertation on Spinoza, *Le bonheur de Spinoza* (published in 1944 and 1946 in the issues 39 and 41 of *La Revue de Métaphysique et de Morale*). In 1943 he engaged in the partisan war in the Lyon region. In 1945 he passed the *agrégation*. Between 1945 and 1960 he was a researcher attached to the Thiers Foundation and then to the CNRS [*Centre National de la Recherche Scientifique*]. In 1954 he published his first novel, *Le Jeune officier*. Starting from 1960 he began teaching at the University of Montpellier. In 1965, he defended his two dissertations, *Philosophy and Phenomenology of the Body*, supervised by Jean Wahl, and *The Essence of Manifestation*, supervised by Jean Hyppolite, who became a close friend. In 1965, because

The German Ideology was on the *agrégation*'s program, Michel Henry began reading Marx. His interpretation of Marx would be published in two volumes in 1976.

MICHEL FOUCAULT

Born on 15 October 1924 in Poitiers, Foucault studied at *Henri IV* secondary school and in 1946 entered the *Ecole Normale Supérieure*. He obtained an undergraduate degree in psychology in 1947 and in 1949, under the supervision of Jean Hyppolite, he wrote his DES [*diplôme d'études supérieures*] dissertation on *The Constitution of a Historical Transcendental in Hegel's Phenomenology of Spirit*. Foucault passed his *agrégation* in 1951. From 1953 until 1955, he taught psychology at the *Ecole Normale* and at the University of Lille. His first publication is the 1954 "Foreword" to the translation of Ludwig Binswanger's *Traum und Existenz* and the book *Maladie mentale et personnalité*, commissioned by Louis Althusser, who had been the teacher and a good friend of Foucault during their days together at the *Ecole Normale*. From 1955 to 1959 he served as director of the French Institute in Uppsala and then in Warsaw. In 1960 he defended his two Ph.D. dissertations on Kant's *Pragmatic Anthropology*, supervised by Hyppolite, and on *Madness and Culture*, supervised by Canguilhem. From 1960 to 1969 he taught psychology at the University of Clermont-Ferrand. In 1964 he published *The Birth of the Clinic* and in 1966 *The Order of Things*, texts central to the discussion within the *Cahiers pour l'analyse* group. In 1969 he was appointed as professor at the University of Vincennes. During the mid-60s, he participated, with Jules Vuillemin and other intellectuals, in the scientific commission gathered by the French minister of education Christian Fouchet to elaborate a reform of secondary and academic education that would be the object of several student contestations starting from November 1967.

MICHEL SERRES

Born on 1 September 1930 in Agen, Serres entered Brest's *Ecole Navale* in 1949 and then the *Ecole Normale Supérieure* in 1952 where he obtained his *agrégation* in 1955. From 1956 to 1958 he served in the French Navy and, later, was a lecturer at the *Ecole Normale*. During the 60s he taught at the University of Clermont-Ferrand. In this period, Serres wrote and published many articles on themes ranging from seventeenth-century French theatre to the historical and philosophical evaluation of mathematics from the Greeks to the modern period. In 1968 he defended his Ph.D. dissertation, supervised by Jean Hyppolite, entitled *Le système de Leibniz et ses modèles mathématiques*. He would later join the philosophy department of the University of Vincennes.

ALAIN BADIOU
Born in 1937 in Rabat (Morocco), Badiou studied at Fermat secondary school in Toulouse and then at *Louis Le Grand* secondary school in Paris before entering the *Ecole Normale Supérieure* in 1956. In 1960 he passed the agrégation, the following year he began teaching in Reims secondary school. After two years of military service, in 1963, he began teaching philosophy at the University of Reims. Initially fascinated by Sartre, he finished writing his first novel, *Almagestes*, in 1959. At the beginning of the 60s he began reading Lacan and Lévi-Strauss at the suggestion of Louis Althusser. In 1966 he got closer to Althusser, who invited him to give a seminar on literature (*"L'autonomie du processus esthétique"*); at the same time he wrote a review of *For Marx* and of *Reading Capital* (*"Le (re)commencement du matérialisme dialectique"*). In 1966, his friend François Regnault invited him to join the *Cahiers pour l'analyse*, a journal led by a group of Althusserian and Lacanian students, where he published two articles (*"La subversion infinitésimale"* and *"Marque et manque: à propos du zero"*). On the eve of the events of May 1968 Badiou wrote his *Concept of Model*, conceived for Althusser's philosophy seminar for scientists. He was appointed professor at the University of Vincennes' Experimental Centre in 1969.

APPENDIX B

The critical value of images

Alain Badiou (1993)[1]

Regardless of the sophisticated forms of televisual technology, it remains conditioned by a single problem: what does the body in its manifest presence bring to philosophical signification? What could be the privilege of an effectively incarnated speech? From this point of view the variations remain necessarily limited: it always concerns body as sign. This is not the body as general sign but as an encircled sign and the singularity of a language. Having made the body a sign is perhaps the essential contribution of cinema, that is to say, to explore this space of infinite meaning that is the body, considered not only as the source of action but as sign and also as a language. Cinema as the art of body-language, this is perhaps one of its best definitions. And much time will have to pass no doubt before we could fully employ the possibilities offered up by the perception of the image of a face and of a speaking person.

But when it concerns filmed or televised philosophy, we need to remember that philosophy is primordially and originally linguistic. How are these two dimensions to be articulated? How is philosophy-language to be served by body-language? Is there a sort of redoubling of the function of sign? It is first that of the meaning of the question asked of the relation of image and language, at least when it concerns this signifying encircling of speech which is the presence of the body, the face, and the gestures that supports it.

But if philosophy is primordially and originally linguistic, we are also drawn to ask if the transformation of philosophical speech, when it is deployed in the technical space of television, is not an adulteration or even, as we say, whether speech does not end up being devoured by the image, bogged down by it, and stripped of its proper meaning, obscured and reduced to a sort of simple sonic accompaniment that brings forth only from time to time some rare fragments of meaning.

I would respond to this that the image can have a properly philosophical function to speech that I would a critical function.

We need, in effect, to distinguish three syntaxes that were juxtaposed in these broadcasts. One is a properly speaking "syntax" of philosophical rationality, then a gestural and corporeal "syntax" that supports it, and finally a cinematographic "syntax" whose function is to reveal the first two. Usually when we see someone speak we immediately perceive the adherence between gesture and discourse. The function of television is to show us, not the massive evidence of this concrete relation, but its difficulties and even its dialectics. An isolated gesture, filmed for itself, could reveal the reticence of a body with regard to the speech that had just been pronounced, a tension between the existence that manifests in the body, of the body of the philosopher, and the order of thought that is in the process of developing. The proper task of television is to show us that all thought is the thought of an existence and this is not a simply given but rather a latent contradiction that renders the order of signs shown through the body not a pre-established harmony like the order of signs deployed in language. In other words, the bogging down of speech in image is not necessarily like a trial of the image in its valorization of speech. It could also be a sort of critique of speech. The image analyzed by the camera could reveal all that the speaker does not adhere to in discourse. It thus offers a sort of immediate critical reflection. In this regard, philosophical television might not only be the presentation of an incarnation of discourse but [also] the critique of discourse. But for this critical function to be fully exercised we need for philosophy not only to be on the side of what is seen but also on the side of one who sees, that is to say on the two sides of the camera.

Note

1 This short essay reflecting on the television project almost thirty years before was prepared on the occasion of a retrospective on the project as a whole by the *Cahiers philosophiques* journal published in June 1993. Alain Badiou, "Valeur critique des images," *Cahiers philosophiques*, 55 (June 1993): 120–1.

INDEX

Alain (Emile Chartier) 153
Alquié, Ferdinand xxvii,
    11–12n. 1
Althusser, Louis xi, xiv, xvi,
    xxviii, xxii–xxiv, xxv–
    xxxviii, xln. 24, xliiin. 45,
    xlivn. 64, xlvin. 88,
    xlviin. 95, ln. 133, 30n. 14,
    45n. 1, 157–8
Anaximander 117–18
Archimedes 117–18
Aristotle xxxv, 6, 12n. 3, 35, 65,
    75n. 4, 83, 91, 129
Aron, Raymond vii, xxii, xxvii,
    xxxi–xxxii, 33–46, 139–43,
    153
Aubenque, Pierre 12n. 3

Bachelard, Gaston xxxiii, 18, 22,
    28nn. 2, 3, 30n. 14, 71,
    77n. 12, 82, 94n. 6, 120,
    122, 136n. 9, 137n. 13,
    153
Bachelard, Suzanne xviii,
    xlivn. 57
Badiou, Françoise xliiin. 55
Badiou, Raymond xiii, 153
Balibar, Etienne xxv
Baring, Edward xvi, xliiin. 46,
    xlv. 80
Barthes, Roland xix–xxi, xxviii,
    xlvn. 69, 70, 75n. 2
Beaufret, Jean xxii–xxiii

Beauvoir, Simone de x, xiii,
    xxxixn. 5, xl. 15
Benoît Chantre xxxvi
Bergson, Henri xxxii–xxxiii,
    xxxvii, xlvin. 84, 29n. 5,
    73, 109n. 1, 154
Birault, Henri xxii–xxiii
Blüwal, Marcel 129, 135n. 1,
    138n. 26
Bohr, Niels 119–20, 122,
    137n. 13
Borreil, Jean ix–x, xxxviii
Bosteels, Bruno xliiin. 48,
    xlviiin. 102, 108
Boulez, Pierre xxii
Bourbaki, Nicolas xiii, xvii, 17,
    21, 29n. 4
Bourdieu, Pierre xvi, xxiii, xxx,
    xxxiii, xlixnn. 119, 120, 121,
    122, 125, 45n. 1, 109n. 5
Brunschvicg, Leon xxxiii, 76n. 9
Butor, Michel xx

Calvino, Italo xx
Canguilhem, Georges x, xii–
    xiii, xviii–xix, xxii–xxiii,
    xxv, xxvii–xxviii, xxx,
    xxxii, xxxiv, xlivn. 67,
    xlvinn. 86, 89, 15–31,
    46n. 7, 59n. 2, 62, 79–82,
    84–5, 90, 97n. 1, 98n. 6,
    100, 136n. 8, 139–40, 146,
    148–50, 151n. 2, 153, 156

Cartan, Henri xl. 11
Castoriadis, Cornelius xxxixn. 3
Cavaillès, Jean xviii, xix, xxxiii, xlivnn. 62, 66, 67
Chaplin Matheson, Tamara xxix, xlviiin. 113, xlixn. 116
Châtelet, Gilles x, xvi
Chérif Sahli, Mohamed xv, xliin. 42.
Chevalley, Claude xln. 11
Clément, Cathérine x, xxv, xxxixn. 9
Cohen, Jean xv, xliin. 42
Comte, Comte 15, 28n. 1, 35, 46n. 7, 52n. 2
Coulomb, Jean xln. 11
Cousin, Victor xxviii, 11n. 1, 59n. 2
Crick, Francis 136n. 8
Cusset, Francois x, xxxviin. 2

De Gaulle, Charles xiii
Deleuze, Gilles xiii, xv–xvi, xxviii, xxxviiin. 13, 155
Delsarte, Jean xln. 11
Derrida, Jacques x, xvii–xviii, xxi, xxviii, xliiin. 46, xlvn. 80, 110n. 6, 155
Descartes 2–3, 5, 6, 12n. 5, 27, 30n. 11, 58, 73, 79, 88, 91, 94, 147
Dieudonné, Jean xln. 11
Dilthey, Wilhem 57, 60n. 8, 67, 65n. 6
Dosse, François xliiin. 50
Dreyfus, Dina x, xi, xxvii–xxviii, xxx, xxxiv–xxxvi, xxxviii, xlviiin. 111, xlixn. 119, 34, 48, 62, 79, 83, 100, 139, 151n. 1, 154
Dugas, René François 21, 30n. 13
Duhem, Pierre 21, 30n. 12, 127

Durkheim, Emile 40–1, 46nn. 4, 5, 6, 10, 109n. 5
Duroux, Yves xxxiii

Ehresmann, Charles xln. 11
Eichenbaum, Boris 137n. 17
Emile Heriot xx
Establet, Roger xxv

Fabiani, Jean-Louis xxviii, xlviiinn. 112, 114, 115
Faye, Jean-Pierre xxi
Flèchet, Jean xxix
Foucault, Michel xii, xvi, xxi, xxviii, xlvin. 89, xlviiin. 110, 34, 47–60, 62, 79–80, 82, 84–5, 97n. 3, 98n. 4, 110n. 6, 139, 141, 143, 145, 154, 156
Fouchet, Christian xxx, 156
France, Pierre-Mendes xiii
François Regnault xi, xlvn. 67, 157
Freud, Sigmund 52, 54–7, 75n. 3, 76n. 7, 77n. 12, 126, 155

Gide, André 109n. 1
Gilson, Etienne 98n. 10
Goémé, Christine xln. 16, xlin. 26
Goldschmidt, Victor xxii, xlvn. 63
Gracq, Julien x, xxxixn. 9
Granger, Gilles-Gaston xxiii, xix, xlvn. 58, 60
Greimas, Algirdas Julien 75n. 2
Grenel, Gérard xiii, xv, xvi
Grenier, Jean 156
Grothendieck, Alexander xxxii
Guéhenno, Jean 156
Gueroult, Martial xix, xxviii, xlvn. 63, 65, 8, 12nn. 1, 5, 7, 13 n. 7, 98n. 10
Guiraud, Pierre 77n. 15

Hallward, Peter xln. 13, xlivn. 67, xlviin. 96
Hegel xxi–xxii, xxxiv–xxxvi, xlin. 25, 2, 6, 10, 12nn. 2, 6, 51, 96, 154
Heidegger, Martin xvi, xxi, xxii–xxiii, xxxv, xxxviii, xlvn. 75, 12nn. 3, 4, 49, 75n. 5, 92nn. 2, 3, 145, 154
Henry, Michel xxviii, xxxvi–xxxvii, xxxviiin. 110, 99–110
Heraclitus xxxv
Hesiod 67
Heurgon, Marc xln. 12
Homer 67
Husserl, Edmund xviii, xlivnn. 57, 61, 109–10n. 6, 155
Hyppolite, Jean viii, x, xii, xviii, xxxixxii, xxv, xxvii–xxviii, xxx, xxxv–xxxvi, xlvnn. 75, 76, xlviiinn. 109, 110, xlixn. 119, 1–13, 12 n. 2, n. 5 and n.7, 79, 81–2, 84–8, 94, 97–8, 97nn. 2, 3, 98nn. 7, 9, 100, 136n. 8, 141–2, 146–9, 154, 156, 157

Jacob, François 136n. 8
Jakobson, Roman 137n. 17
Jalley, Emile xxiii, xlin. 28, xlvnn. 76, 76, xlvin. 87
Janicaud, Dominique 75n. 75
Jaspers, Karl 156
Jeanson, Francis xv

Kant, Immanuel xlviiin. 110, 2, 3, 10, 12, 29n. 9, 50, 51, 53, 73, 76n. 9, 84, 88, 89, 90, 94, 97n. 3, 141, 147, 156
Kekulé, August 120

Kelvin, William Thomson 123
Kepler, Johannes 27, 117, 118
Khodoss, Forence xlviiin. 111
Koyré, Alexandre 28n. 3

Lacan, Jacques xi, xxi–xxvi, xxviii, xlixn. 130, 55, 59n. 7, 75n. 2, 76n. 7, 126, 137n. 19, 157
Lachelier, Jules 76n. 9
Lagache, Daniel xxiii, xlvin. 83, 59n. 2, 153
Lagneau, Jules 76n. 9
Lanzmann, Claude xiii
Laplanche, Jean xxii, xxiv, xlvn. 81, xlviin. 94, xlixn. 119
Lautman, Albert xxviii, xix, xxxv
Lazarsfeld, Paul Felix 41, 46n. 9
Leclaire, Serge xxiv, xlviin. 94
Lefort, Claude xxiv, xlvin. 91
Leibniz, Gottfried Wilhelm xviii, xlviiin. 110, xlixn. 128, 2, 20, 29 n. 8, 112, 135n. 5, 157
Lemaître, Georges 118
Lévi-Strauss, Claude xvii, xxi, xxiv, xxvii–xxviii, xxxiii, xliii. 49, 50, 53, 54, xlvin. 92, 29n. 4, 39, 40, 46n. 3, 75n. 2, 125, 126, 134n. 1, 135n.2, 136n. 8, 137n. 18, 156, 158
Lévy-Bruhl, Lucien 46n. 10, 109n. 5
Lwoff, André 136n. 8
Lyotard, Jean-François xxxviiin. 3

Macherey, Pierre xxv, xlvin. 89
Maine de Biran, François, Pierre-Gonthier 59n. 2, 76n. 9
Martin, Roger xviii, xlivn. 62
Martinet, André 70, 77nn. 11, 14

Marx, Karl xxi, xxiii, xln. 24, 35, 37, 38, 51, 143, 154, 156, 157
Matieu, Maurice xvii, xliiin. 56
Mauss, Marcel 128, 138n. 24
Merleau-Ponty, Maurice xiii, xviii, xxv, xxvii, xln. 15, xlin. 31, 54, 59n. 7, 154
Metzger, Hélène 136n. 11
Meyerson, Emile 28n. 1, 29n. 5
Meyerson, Ignace xxiii
Michaux, Henri 127, 138n. 22
Mill, John Stuart 41
Miller, Jean-Claude xxxii
Molière, Jean-Baptiste Poquelin 128, 129, 135, 138
Mollet, Guy xvi
Monod, Jacques 136

Nabert, Jean 76n. 9
Nietzsche, Friedrich xxxvii, xxxviiin. 3, 38, 53, 57, 89, 98, 103, 105
Nora, Pierre xliiin. 50

Passeron, Jean-Claude xxiii, xxx, xlixnn. 120, 121, 122, 125
Perec, Georges xx
Perse, Saint-John xlviin. 99
Picasso, Pablo 93
Plato xxviii, 2, 3, 5, 6, 10, 11, 63, 64, 65, 69, 73, 94, 135n. 4, 147
Politzer, Georges xxii, xxiii, xxv, 54, 59n. 7, 76n. 7
Possel, René de xln. 11
Propp, Vladimir 137n. 17

Queneau, Raymond xx

Radcliffe-Brown 40
Rancière, Jacques xxv, xlviin. 97

Ricoeur, Paul xviii, xxii, xxiv, xxvii–xxviii, xlviin. 93, 34, 48, 61–77, 75nn. 2, 3, 5, 76nn. 7, 8, 9, 77n. 12, 80, 82–3, 100, 110n. 6, 142–9, 155
Robbe-Grillet, Alain xx, xxi, xlvn. 71
Rousseau, Jean-Jacques x

Sarraute, Nathalie xx
Sartre, Jean-Paul x, xiii–xix, xxi, xxiii–xxix, xxxii, xxviiin. 3, xxxixn. 7, xlnn. 15, 20, 22, 23, 24, xlinn. 31, 32, xliinn 39, 40, 44, xlvn. 68, 41, 43, 59n. 7, 98nn. 8 , 9, 109n. 1, 110n. 8, 153, 154, 157
Saussure, Ferdinand de 64, 70, 72, 75n. 2, 76n. 10
Senghor, Léopold xlin. 32
Serres, Michel xviii, xxii, xxvii–xxviii, xlviiin. 110, 111–38, 135nn. 3, 5, 136n. 10, 137nn. 12, 14, 16, 138nn. 21, 23, 157
Shakespeare, William 8
Shklovsky, Viktor 137n. 17
Simonin, Anne xlvn. 71
Sirinelli, Jean-François xliiin. 47
Sollers, Philippe xxi, xlvn. 72
Spinoza, Benedictus xix, xxxi, xlivn. 67, 2, 3, 155

Taddéï, Frédéric xxxixn. 4, xln. 14
Talcott Parsons 36
Tannery, Paul 21, 30n. 11
Terray, Emmanuel xv, xvii, xix, xxii, xxv, xlnn. 17, 23, xliin. 37, xliiin. 52, xlvn. 68
Tournier, Michel xiii, xv, xvi

Tynyanov, Yury 137n. 17

Ullmann, Stephen 77n. 16

Vermeren, Patrice xln. 23
Verstraeten, Pierre xv, xviii, xxv,
    xln. 17, xliiinn. 53, 56
Vidal-Naquet, Pierre xxxviiin. 3
Voltaire, François-Marie
    Arouet x

Vuillemin, Jules xviii, xxii,
    xlivnn. 59, 60, 156

Watson, James D. 136n. 8
Weber, Max 36, 41, 46n. 8
Weil, André xvii, 29n. 4
Weil, Simone 29n. 4
Wolff, Christian 20–1, 29n. 9

Zola, Émile 136n. 6